Contents

Summary

'As a casual worker, I do not get a bonus, or paid holiday or severance pay. I am looking for a place to stay so that I can collect all my children to stay with me. To be a mother with my chickens under my wings.'[1]
Ragel, picking fruit in South Africa for export to UK supermarkets

'We have to do overtime until midnight to earn a decent income. I am afraid of having children because I wouldn't be able to feed them.'[2]
Nong, 26, sewing underwear for Victoria's Secret in Thailand

'We don't have the right to be sick. One day when I was not well and I took a doctor's note to my employer, he gave me a written warning.'[3]
Zakia, 36, sewing garments for Spain's El Corte Inglés in Morocco

Globalisation has drawn millions of women into paid employment across the developing world. Today, supermarkets and clothing stores source the products that they sell from farms and factories worldwide. At the end of their supply chains, the majority of workers – picking and packing fruit, sewing garments, cutting flowers – are women. Their work is fuelling valuable national export growth. And their jobs could be providing the income, security, and support needed to lift them and their families out of poverty. Instead, women workers are systematically being denied their fair share of the benefits brought by globalisation.

Commonly hired on short-term contracts – or with no contract at all – women are working at high speed for low wages in unhealthy conditions. They are forced to put in long hours to earn enough to get by. Most have no sick leave or maternity leave, few are enrolled in health or unemployment schemes, and fewer still have savings for the future. Instead of supporting long-term development, trade is reinforcing insecurity and vulnerability for millions of women workers.

The harsh reality faced by women workers highlights one of the glaring failures of the current model of globalisation. Over the past 20 years, the legal rights of powerful corporate entities have been dramatically deepened and extended. Through the World Trade Organization and regional and bilateral trade agreements, corporations now enjoy global protection for many newly introduced rights. As investors, the same companies are legally protected against a wide range of governments' actions. Workers' rights have moved in the opposite direction. And it is no coincidence that the rise of the 'flexible' worker has been accompanied by the rise of the female, often migrant, worker.
The result is that corporate rights are becoming ever stronger, while poor people's rights and protections at work are being weakened, and women are paying the social costs.

Exploiting the circumstances of vulnerable people – whether intentionally or not – is at the heart of many employment strategies in global supply chains. Of course vulnerable social groups desperately need employment as a means of escaping poverty and inequality. But it is no escape at all if the way that they are employed turns their vulnerability into an opportunity for employers to pay them less, work them harder and longer, and avoid paying their rightful benefits.

The result is a gradual but fundamental shift in who will gain from trade under the current model of globalisation. The benefits of flexibility for companies at the top of global supply chains have come at the cost of precarious employment for those at the bottom. If this is to be the future of export-oriented employment, trade will fall far short of its potential for poverty reduction and gender equality.

Oxfam's research with partners in 12 countries involved interviews with hundreds of women workers and many farm and factory managers, supply chain agents, retail and brand company staff, unions and government officials. It has revealed how retailers (supermarkets and department stores) and clothing brands are using their power in supply chains systematically to push many costs and risks of business on to producers, who in turn pass them on to working women. Chapter 1 sets out the impacts of this trend on women workers and their families:

- In Chile, 75 per cent of women in the agricultural sector are hired on temporary contracts picking fruit, and put in more than 60 hours a week during the season. But one in three still earns below the minimum wage.

- Fewer than half of the women employed in Bangladesh's textile and garment export sector have a contract, and the vast majority get no maternity or health coverage – but 80 per cent fear dismissal if they complain.

- In China's Guangdong province, one of the world's fastest growing industrial areas, young women face 150 hours of overtime each month in the garment factories – but 60 per cent have no written contract and 90 per cent have no access to social insurance.

The impacts of such precarious employment go far beyond the workplace. Most women are still expected to raise children and care for sick and elderly relatives when they become cash-earners. They are doubly burdened, and, with little support from their governments or employers to cope with it, the stress can destroy their own health, break up their families, and undermine their children's chances of a better future. The result: the very workers who are the backbone of wealth creation in many developing countries are being robbed of their share of the gains that trade could bring.

The impacts are felt by workers in both rich and poor countries. Women and migrants from poor communities in rich countries – such as US and Canadian agricultural workers and UK and Australian home-based workers – likewise face precarious terms of employment in trade-competing sectors. The pressure of competition from low-cost imports is clearly one reason, but so too is the pressure inherent in being employed at the end of a major company's global supply chain, whether it is sourcing overseas or domestically.

One cause of such precarious conditions is the new business model that has emerged under globalisation, described in chapter 2. Retail and brand companies have positioned themselves as powerful gatekeepers between the world's consumers and producers. Their global supply chains stretch from the supermarket shelves and clothes rails in the world's major shopping centres to the fruit and vegetable farms of Latin America and Africa and the garment factories of South Asia and China. Wal-Mart, the world's biggest retailer, has driven this model, buying products from 65,000 suppliers worldwide and selling to over 138 million consumers every week through its 1,300 stores in 10 countries.

Globalisation has hugely strengthened the negotiating hand of retailers and brand companies. New technologies, trade liberalisation, and capital mobility have dramatically opened up the number of countries and producers from which they can source their products, creating a growing number of producers vying for a place in their supply chains. At the same time, international mergers and acquisitions and aggressive pricing strategies have concentrated market power in the hands of a few major retailers, now building international empires. These companies have tremendous power in their negotiations with producers and they use that power to push the costs and risks of business down the supply chain. Their business model, focused on maximising returns for shareholders, demands increasing flexibility through 'just-in-time' delivery, but tighter control over inputs and standards, and ever-lower prices.

Under such pressures, factory and farm managers typically pass on the costs and risks to the weakest links in the chain: the workers they employ. For many producers, their labour strategy is simple: make it flexible and make it cheap. Faced with fluctuating orders and falling prices, they hire workers on short-term contracts, set excessive targets, and sub-contract to sub-standard, unseen producers. Pressured to meet tight turnaround times, they demand that workers put in long hours to meet shipping deadlines. And to minimise resistance, they hire workers who are less likely to join trade unions (young women, often migrants and immigrants) and they intimidate or sack those who do stand up for their rights.

Governments should be strengthening protection for workers in the face of these intense commercial pressures. Instead many have traded away workers' rights, in law or in practice. Under pressure from local and foreign investors and from IMF and World Bank loan conditions, they have too often allowed labour standards to be defined by the demands of supply chain flexibility: easier hiring and firing, more short-term contracts, fewer benefits, and longer periods of overtime. It brings a short-term advantage for trade, but at the risk of a long-term cost to society.

Companies increasingly hold up their 'codes of conduct' to assure the public that they care about labour standards down the chain. But their farm and factory audits still focus on documenting the labour problems that exist, without asking why those problems persist. Many factors can contribute – from poor management to weak national legislation. But one root cause, long overlooked, is the pressures of retailers' and brand companies' own supply-chain purchasing practices, undermining the very labour standards that they claim to support.

Anyone appalled by 'sweat shop' conditions in garment factories should be asking: who turned up the heat? The pressure on workers starts far from the factory floor – coming down the supply chain through retailers' and brands' strategies, as described in chapter 3. Their demands for 'just-in-time' delivery have typically cut production times by 30 per cent in five years – coupled with smaller, less predictable orders and high airfreight costs for missed deadlines. Moroccan factories producing for Spain's major department store, El Corte Inglés, must turn orders round in less than seven days. *'The shops always need to be full of new designs,'* said one production planning manager, *'We pull out all the stops to meet the deadline ... Our image is on the line.'* But the image they hide is of young women working up to 16 hours a day to meet those deadlines, underpaid by 40 per cent for their long overtime working. *'There's a girl who's seven months pregnant working ten hours a day,'* said one garment worker, *'and as she has to make a lot of pieces per hour the employer doesn't let her go to the toilet. It's sheer torture for her, but she can't afford to lose her job.'*

Across countries, falling prices (for many garment producers, by 30 per cent over three years) increase the pressure to cut costs; sub-contracting to workshops with far worse conditions is a popular but hidden solution. And when buyers make no promise of future orders, their calls to improve labour standards ring hollow. No wonder that many managers falsify records and intimidate workers to answer questions 'correctly'.

The fresh produce industry – fruit, vegetables, and flowers – is inherently risky, but supermarkets' tough negotiations can increase that gamble. As chapter 4 shows, farmers across the world are made to carry the costs and risks when supermarkets set prices long after the produce has been shipped, when they demand exclusive relationships but then drop the order, and when they run cut-price promotions to achieve their own sales targets. *'The only ham left in the sandwich is our labour costs,'* said one South African apple farmer exporting to the UK's biggest supermarket, Tesco. *'If they squeeze us, it's the only place where we can squeeze'.* Little wonder that farmers like him are increasingly hiring women on temporary contracts to work 11 hours a day in the fields for poverty wages, with no sick leave, no maternity leave, and no income security.

Time to make trade fair

As part of Oxfam's campaign to Make Trade Fair, we are joining partner organisations worldwide to demand that women working in the supply chains of some of the world's most powerful companies get their fair share of the gains from trade. Their experiences and struggles are at the heart of this report and our international campaigning. Together we are calling for:

- Companies – retailers and brands – to make respect for labour rights integral to their supply-chain business strategies, especially by addressing the impacts of their own sourcing and purchasing practices on the way that producers hire and treat their workers

- Producers and suppliers worldwide to provide decent jobs for their employees, including respect for workers' right to join trade unions and bargain collectively, and eliminating discrimination against women workers

- National governments, South and North, to stop trading away workers' rights in law and in practice, and to enforce international labour standards in order to promote decent employment for poverty reduction, gender equality, and development

- The IMF and World Bank to promote workers' rights throughout their operations as a fundamental tool for poverty reduction and greater gender equality

- Institutional investors – shareholders and pension funds – to use their power in investment markets to promote supply-chain practices that respect international labour standards

- Consumers to insist that retailers and brands ensure that their sourcing and purchasing practices support, rather than undermine, workers' rights

Introduction

Globalisation conjures up images of multinational companies, flows of investment and technology, and disputes at the World Trade Organisation (WTO). But such images tell only part of the story. Globalisation also has a more human, and more hidden, face. International trade has drawn millions of women into employment across the developing world. They are producing the goods that are fuelling export growth – yet they are systematically denied a fair share of the benefits brought by globalisation.

It is not inevitable that globalisation marginalises the poor in general, or poor women in particular. Nor is it inevitable that the expansion of international trade creates a 'race to the bottom', with investors taking advantage of opportunities to relocate. Increased trade and improved working conditions *can* go hand-in-hand, *if* governments, companies, and international institutions create the right policy conditions.

That *if* is a very big one. As the research set out here shows, powerful political and commercial pressures are undermining labour standards. Governments in many countries are actively eroding labour rights, often on the profoundly mistaken assumption that it is necessary in order to attract foreign investment and fuel growth. In many cases they have been actively encouraged to move in this direction through IMF and World Bank loan conditions.

The rolling back of labour rights has coincided with the rolling out of the new business model. For their part, big retailers, brand companies, and international investors have actively encouraged the development of 'flexible' labour markets – that is, weaker labour rights – to fit their business needs. The flexibility demanded by that business model – for faster delivery, more exacting technical standards, and lower prices, but no commitment to future orders – is in stark contrast to the high-sounding principles endorsed by companies under the banner of corporate social responsibility.

The current emphasis on adapting labour markets to the dictates of a business model that is spreading vulnerability is shortsighted on three counts. First, and most importantly, improving employment and working conditions would create immediate and tangible benefits for millions of women, providing a powerful catalyst for reducing poverty. It would help to create a new, more equitable pattern of globalisation. Second, by spreading the benefits of trade and globalisation more widely, it would strengthen the legitimacy of an international trading system that is widely – and rightly – seen as failing the poor. Third, improved conditions in poor countries would create new opportunities for investment and growth. Ensuring that the development of globalisation and improved labour standards for women are complementary would start to create more winners from trade.

Ways ahead, and false debates to leave behind

This report argues that companies need to change their sourcing and purchasing practices, if their commitments to be socially responsible are to be more than empty words. Better sourcing and purchasing practices alone would not lead to decent employment and working conditions, but they are an essential part of the solution, and a part that has so far been largely missing from the debate. This report likewise calls on governments to ensure that poor people benefit from trade by ratifying and implementing international labour standards, extending employment protections to all workers and, especially, creating the space for workers to join unions and bargain collectively without fearing for their jobs.

Some commentators will reject this strategy. In particular, enthusiasts for the current pattern of globalisation will argue that more of the same is needed to generate higher growth, increased employment, rising living standards, and ultimately improved labour standards. The arguments that they put forward are well known.

1 'Trade and growth first, labour standards will follow'

Trade creates jobs – so the reasoning goes – and as the excess supply of labour falls, wages and working conditions rise. But the link between trade and economic growth is far from automatic, or that between job creation and better labour conditions. Markets may play a critical role in defining the efficiency of resource allocation and generating growth, but market realism has to be tempered with considerations of social justice. Labour rights are not a distant reward of development: they are an essential tool for alleviating poverty through trade today.

2 'Jobs in trade are better than the alternatives'

Many economists point out that export-sector workers already tend to earn higher wages than other workers, let alone the unemployed. A woman in Bangladesh sewing clothes for Wal-Mart, so the argument runs, is surely better off than her sister working on a local construction site. In the words of the economist Paul Krugman, 'In praise of cheap labour: bad jobs at bad wages are better than no jobs at all.'[4] True: and that is why millions of women take these jobs. But if the best deal that trade can offer to poor people is a marginal improvement over a life of desperate poverty, it is falling far short of its potential. The relevant question is not whether the Bangladeshi woman is marginally better off but whether she, her family, and her country are getting a fair share of the gains that she helps to generate through trade.

3 'Improving labour standards is hidden protectionism'

Some claim that improving employment security and benefits for workers in poor countries will take away their trade advantage and price them out of the market. From this perspective, calling for respect for workers' rights is just another variety of Northern protectionism. This is a weak argument. The cost of providing basic benefits such as maternity and sick leave differs hugely across rich and poor countries. If all countries provided these benefits, relative costs of labour would still be far lower in poor countries. And workers' organisations in many poor countries are driving the demands for these rights at work to be respected – not to protect Northern jobs but rather to protect their own well-being, health, and dignity. Universal respect for basic rights at work need not adversely affect the competitive position of low-income countries.

4 'Strengthening rights will cut jobs'

Some fear that better wages and benefits will mean fewer jobs, leaving communities worse off. Not necessarily so: governments hoping to win investment on the basis of low wages have an out-of-date strategy. 'Forget about cheap labour,' advises David Birnbaum, an expert on global garment-sourcing trends. 'Poverty is no longer an asset. There is always some new garment-exporting country where workers earn less than yours.'[5] Low wages and insecure jobs perpetuate poverty in poor communities. When women are better paid and protected in their jobs, they can invest in their families, sending their children to school rather than into the factory or fields to work. It helps to build a more productive and skilled workforce – and that *does* attract investors. All this could help to stimulate domestic and regional sources of consumer demand. In other words, shared prosperity is good for investment – poverty is not.

5 'More secure jobs undermine flexibility'

Proponents of flexible labour laws (encouraging short-term contracts and easy hiring and firing) argue that they are essential to allow firms to respond to fluctuations in demand. True: seasonal fluctuations mean that labour requirements vary through the year, and employers need to be able to adjust. But 'flexibility' is hugely abused in order to secure the long-term effort of workers at short-term costs. Employers in the North and South misuse short-term contracts to avoid paying employment benefits and to undermine workers' bargaining power in organising. Retail and brand buyers exacerbate the problem by changing orders at short notice and pushing for prices that cannot cover the full costs of stable employees. Flexibility matters – but social justice considerations should set limits to the level of flexibility demanded, especially in unequal economic relationships.

6 'Monitoring labour standards throughout supply chains is asking the impossible'

Retail and brand companies are the first to claim that their long and complex supply chains are too complex to monitor. But they already achieve exacting technical, product safety, quality, and delivery standards through those chains. And many leading companies are cutting out layers of mid-chain suppliers and sourcing more directly from producers. This creates the ideal opportunity for working with producers to ensure that good labour standards are met.

Oxfam and partners: campaigning to make trade fair

Oxfam has worked for many years with partner organisations around the world who (often in collaboration with trade unions) support workers – mostly women – employed in global supply chains. Together we have conducted research in twelve countries, North and South, to understand the causes behind the precarious situation of these workers. The research, conducted in Bangladesh, China, Chile, Colombia, Honduras, Kenya, Morocco, South Africa, Sri Lanka, Thailand, the United Kingdom, and the United States, focused on two main sectors: garment supply chains to major clothing retailers and clothing brands, and fresh-produce supply chains to food retailers and the fast-food industry.

The research documented the experiences not only of women workers, but also of their employers, the managers and owners of farms and factories. These latter voices are rarely reported, but understanding the supply-chain pressures that they face as producers is essential to understand why, as employers, they hire and treat workers in the ways that they do.

In all, the research included interviews and surveys with 1,310 workers, 95 garment factory owners and managers, 33 farm and plantation owners and managers, 48 government officials, 98 representatives of unions and non-government organisations (NGOs), 52 importers, exporters, and other supply chain agents, and 17 representatives of brand and retail companies. We have changed the names of all the farm and factory workers interviewed to protect their identity, because many feared that they would lose their jobs for speaking out. We have also kept confidential the identity of the farm and factory managers and exporters and importers interviewed, because many likewise feared losing their place in the supply chains of major retailers and brands. Some staff members of retail and brand companies were also willing to be interviewed only under conditions of anonymity.

Many well-known retail and brand companies feature in this report. Practices vary considerably from company to company, and where particular companies are linked to particular criticisms (or indeed specific good practice) we have made this clear. Generalised statements about industry practices should not, however, be taken to refer to any particular company.

1

Employed, yes –
but precariously

Women in Honduras arriving for another long day's work in the garment factories. If proposed labour law reforms are passed, one worker in three could be put on a temporary employment contract, without employment stability, paid leave, or social security.

1 Employed, yes – but precariously

Lucy, a Kenyan mother of two, sews the pockets onto children's jeans destined for Wal-Mart in the United States, the world's most successful retailer. Her factory, based in an export processing zone (EPZ) outside Nairobi, receives erratic, sub-contracted orders and must keep costs low and output high. Early in 2003, when her manager demanded she work non-stop for two days and nights to meet the shipping deadline, her partner walked out, leaving Lucy to raise the children, aged two and 13. *'He said he will come back when the condition of my work is good.'* she said, *'Till today the condition is becoming worse.'*

In May Lucy sold her table, cupboard, and bed so that she could pay the rent. Then she sold the cooking stove to buy her son's school uniform. In June, when orders stopped for eight weeks, so did the pay. Her parents, living in a village 150km north of Nairobi, agreed to take her children, and she has not seen them for six months. *'If this EPZ could be better, and consider us as people, and give us leave and holidays, then I would be able to go and see the children,'* she said.

Production targets are unrealistically high, and Lucy is expected to put in extra hours to meet them. In September she worked 20 hours of overtime but was paid for only six. Talk of trade unions is banned, and the factory atmosphere is intimidating. *'Supervisors abuse us ... If we talk, they say, "Shut your beak. Even a child can do your job."'* She most pities the young female helpers doing the low-skill tasks such as counting and cleaning the garments. *'If you are a helper, you need security,'* she said. *'They are sexually harassed to keep their job. That's why as women we are so oppressed. Because you can't secure your job through the trade union, you have to buy it with sex.'*[1]

Lucy depends on this job. But she and her family should not be forced to pay such a price to keep it. Worldwide, working women like her – making garments, cutting flowers, and picking fruit – are demanding their fair share of the gains from trade. The only asset they have to offer in trade is their labour. This makes a critical test for globalisation: can it create jobs that empower, rather than undermine, women as workers? So far it is failing.

Facing precarious employment

The last 20 years of trade liberalisation have certainly created jobs for millions of women workers, who occupy 60 to 90 per cent of jobs in the labour intensive stages of the clothing and fresh-produce global supply chains. And these jobs are desperately needed by women and their families. *'May God bless the flowers, because they provide us with work,'* say the women working in Colombia's flower greenhouses.[2] *'Even though the salaries are low,'* said Ana, working in a *maquila*, or export-assembly factory, in Honduras, *'the maquilas give us employment – they help us to make ends meet.'*[3] Facing school costs and medical expenses, poor families increasingly depend on earning cash incomes to

Women as percentage of production employees

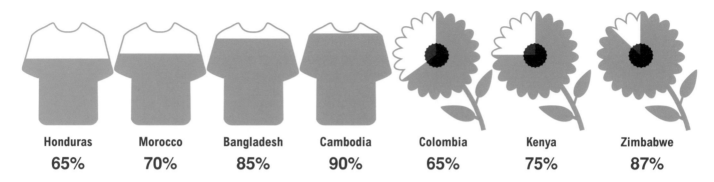

Honduras	Morocco	Bangladesh	Cambodia	Colombia	Kenya	Zimbabwe
65%	**70%**	**85%**	**90%**	**65%**	**75%**	**87%**

Source: Dolan, C and K Sorby (2003) and Oxfam background research reports

meet their most basic needs. Many hope to escape rural poverty, migrating across provinces and countries to do so. And the crisis of HIV and AIDS makes some families all the more dependent on those who can work, increasing the need for their caring work too.

For many individual women, their jobs have brought economic independence, greater equality in the household, and personal empowerment. But the past 20 years have also witnessed the emergence of a new business model, described in chapter 2, based on companies outsourcing production through global supply chains that demand low-cost and 'flexible' labour. In many countries, national labour laws have been weakened or not enforced to accommodate these demands. As a result, millions of women and men at the end of those supply chains are employed precariously:

- insecure: on short-term contracts with limited access to social protection
- exhausted: through working long hours at high pressure in unhealthy conditions
- undermined: in their attempts to organise and demand for their rights to be met.

Precarious employment is far from new – it has long been the reality for poor people, especially in informal sectors in developing countries. Export-sector jobs, connecting them to some of the world's most profitable companies, should be an opportunity for more secure and empowering employment. But instead, the sourcing and purchasing practices of those companies create pressures down the chain which result in precarious conditions. The impact falls on poor communities in rich countries, too, where workers employed in trade-competing sectors – often migrants and immigrants – likewise face precarious conditions. The result is a two-tier labour market, split between those whose standard of living grows with the economy and those employed precariously without minimal protection.

Empowerment through employment in Bangladesh

In 1982 the government of Bangladesh began to promote export-oriented manufacturing; within two years, the garment industry took off. The sight of thousands of young women in the streets of Dhaka travelling to and from work was a highly visible sign of social change. For many, there has been significant personal change too.

Paid employment has improved many women's bargaining power within the family, especially with husbands, fathers, and brothers. A 1990 survey of more than 30 garment factories found that two out of three women had some control over their earnings.[4] According to one woman, '*In my mother's time ... women had to tolerate more suffering because they did not have the means to become independent. They are better off now, they know about the world, they have been given education, they can work and stand on their own feet. They have more freedom.*'[5]

Many married women workers interviewed in 2003 said that they now take decisions with their husbands on family matters, and 13 per cent said their husbands now shared some of the housework, especially shopping and cooking – a small but significant shift in a strongly gendered society.[6] '*The garment sector has brought a silent revolution for women in our society,*' said Shirin Akter of Karmojibi Nari, an NGO supporting women workers. '*But women workers' rights and status will still not be secured until their freedom of association is assured and their voices are more widely heard.*'[7]

Far too much of women's work is still uncounted and undervalued.

International Labour Organization[9]

All poor people face costs when employed in this way, but the impacts fall particularly hard on women:

- Women typically have less education, land, or savings than the men in their families. That weaker negotiating position leaves them with the primary responsibility for caring work in the home – raising children, tending to the sick and elderly – and it makes them more dependent on whatever paid work they can get. No wonder they occupy the vast majority of jobs at the end of global supply chains.

- Stuck in low-skilled, low-paid jobs, women are less able to renegotiate their household roles, and so they bear a double burden of paid and unpaid work. That undermines their struggle for greater equality in the home and in society, and leaves little time for participating in workers' organisations and social support groups.

- Insecure contracts often lack the protections and benefits – such as limits on overtime, rest days, sick leave, accident cover, and maternity leave – that are invaluable for women in supporting their families. Without this support, either from the State or from employers, the strain often undermines their own health and well-being and their children's futures.[8]

The harmful impacts of precarious employment can be long-term and community-wide. And they are felt in every country. Women and migrants from poor communities in rich countries also face precarious terms of employment in trade-competing sectors. The pressure of competition from low-cost imports is clearly one reason – but so too is the pressure inherent in being employed in a global supply chain, whether it is sourcing domestically or overseas.

Permanently temporary

Women are more likely than men to be hired on short-term, seasonal, casual, or homework contracts, renewed every year, every three months, or even every day. They end up working long-term but without the protection and support that come with long-term jobs. In Chile and South Africa, women get the temporary jobs in the fruit sector, hired on 'rolling contracts' for up to 11 months, year after year. *'We are permanent when it suits management,'* as one South African woman put it.[10] Likewise, almost all of China's migrant garment workers are given one-year contracts, repeatedly renewed, leaving them with no job security.

Women are the temporary workers on fruit farms

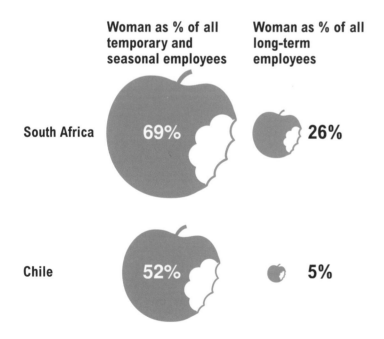

Woman as % of all temporary and seasonal employees

Woman as % of all long-term employees

South Africa   69%   26%

Chile   52%   5%

Source: Barrientos *et al.* (1999) and Venegas (1993) cited in C. Dolan and K Sorby (2003)

It is sometimes assumed that women want such 'flexible' jobs so that they have time to care for their families. When those jobs are well protected under law, women can benefit from having this choice. But for the vast majority of women interviewed, working on short-term contracts is not a choice but a necessity – and is all that they are offered. For home-based workers in the UK (of whom 90 per cent are women and 50 per cent are from ethnic minorities), the supply of work they receive from manufacturers is highly irregular, sometimes with very short deadlines. *'Homeworkers often get no redundancy pay, holiday or sick pay, and no pension,'* said Linda Devereux, Director of the National Group on Homeworking. *'This is not the kind of "flexibility" that any woman worker is hoping for.'* [11] The increasing use of temporary and contract labour is a worrying trend in many countries.

Employed: but who is the employer?

When workers are not formally recognised as employees, they fall outside the protection of labour law. In some countries, having no written contract means having no legal recognition. In Bangladesh, only 46 per cent of women garment workers interviewed had the letter of employment that is needed to establish the employment relationship. No wonder that almost none received pay slips or was enrolled in a health scheme, and the vast majority got no paid maternity leave.[12] Layers of supply chain sub-contracting can blur legal relationships too. In Chile, companies are liable in law if the sub-contractors they use fail to pay sub-contracted workers' wages or benefits – but the law is not always enforced. *'In many cases the company has kept on workers who have not been paid by the farm labour contractor,'* explained Jessica, hired through a contractor to pack grapes for export to the USA. *'The company tells them "But we have paid for all that – it is the farm-labour contractor who has not fulfilled his obligations to you."'*[13]

Little support for families

Paid maternity leave is essential for supporting women as workers and as mothers – and for ensuring the health of the current and future workforce. But women hired on short-term contracts who become pregnant simply do not get their contract renewed, and others with the right in law often cannot claim it in practice. In Kenya, some garment workers seek back-street abortions, losing the baby and risking their own lives in order to save the job. And those who do have children pay the price. *'In my company you lose your work number when you go on maternity,'* explained one young woman. *'This means that, if you are lucky enough to be readmitted, you come back as a new employee, losing all the benefits for the period worked before going on maternity leave.'*[14]

Short-term hiring for long-term jobs

Hiring workers on short-term contracts can be legitimate – for example, for jobs that are genuinely seasonal or temporary in nature. But many employers abuse the law and repeatedly hire workers this way for years. Why? It cuts their costs, avoiding employment benefits. It discourages workers from joining unions, by withholding job security. And it enables employers to expand and contract the workforce to fit fluctuating order levels. But these 'savings' for employers turn into social costs for women and their families. Policy makers may not calculate these costs because they are not monetary, but women know the price of, say, having no sick leave: working when ill or sending sick children off to school.

Indonesia

Since the economic crisis of 1998, the use of short-term contracts has increased significantly. New legislation in 2003 clarified and limited the legitimate uses of such contracts and allows only one renewal. But the limits are not effectively enforced. One network of Indonesian NGOs and unions is documenting just how widespread their misuse has become. Initial findings from six factories in West Java revealed between 15 and 95 per cent of workers were repeatedly hired on short-term contracts, three to 12 months at a time. They are making sports shoes, garments, and metal products – work which is neither temporary nor seasonal by nature.[15]

South Africa

The Confederation of Employers of South Africa, COFESA, shows member companies how to cut labour costs through a legislative loophole: turn employees into 'independent contractors'. This instantly cuts labour costs by 30 per cent and makes employers exempt from obligations under the Labour Relations Act. For garment workers, the switch may mean doing the same work but without the employee protections of a minimum wage and overtime limits, paid leave, or medical and unemployment benefit schemes. COFESA's founder estimates that their advice has helped to turn one and a half million of South Africa's workers into independent contractors – and that the practice will keep spreading. '*The system can work in any industry,*' he said. '*We can always work out something.*'[16]

Colombia

Labour law reforms in 2002 lengthened the workday, cut overtime pay, reduced severance payments, and introduced more flexible contracts. CACTUS, an NGO supporting women working in the flower industry, is concerned that their use may spread throughout the sector. '*With these policies, labour conditions will get worse,*' said Ricardo Zamudio, Director of CACTUS. '*According to the government, these policies of cutting costs for enterprises are intended to create jobs, but they don't guarantee new posts, they just deepen poverty.*'[17]

Honduras

The government's proposed labour reforms would permit garment factories to hire up to 30 per cent of their workers on temporary contracts. If passed, the reforms would save employers US$90m over three years. For workers, that would mean a loss of job security, paid leave, social security, and the annual bonus. An alliance of national unions and NGOs are campaigning to stop this change in the law so that women workers do not lose the support and benefits that they need. '*The majority of people who will be affected by this law will be single mothers, poor people, and migrants,*' said Maria Luisa Regalado of CODEMUH, an NGO in that alliance. '*If they are dismissed, they will be totally unprotected.*'[18]

Stuck at the bottom

In the fruit industry, women are the pickers, sorters, graders, and packers. In the flower industry, they do the weeding, plant tying, pruning, cutting, picking, and packing. In the garment industry, women sew, finish, and pack the clothes. There is skill in doing these jobs fast and well, but they are perceived to be low-skill – and similar to women's tasks at home – so are typically low-paid. Supervisors, machine operators, and technicians tend to be men, earning more. In Colombia's flower farms, for example, technical irrigation systems are managed by men; irrigation with a hose is women's work.[19] Dividing men's and women's roles in this way not only entrenches pay gaps but also reinforces women's subordination. One route to getting better-paid and more secure jobs is training, but few women are ever offered the chance. *'[the farmer] only chooses the men for training,'* said one South African fruit picker. *'Here it is not a woman's thing, it is a man's thing. You remain a general worker, even though you have the knowledge.'*[20]

Low pay, high pressure

Minimum wage levels in many countries are scarcely more than poverty wages – set by what the market will pay, not what families need. As a result, women often cannot earn enough in a basic week's work. In Honduras, garment workers earn above the minimum wage, but the government's own calculations show that the minimum covers only 33 per cent of a family's basic needs.[21] In Bangladesh, 98 per cent of garment workers interviewed were paid at least the minimum wage – but its level was set in 1994, and the price of basic foods has more than doubled since then. Allowing for inflation, one woman in three is effectively earning below the minimum.[22]

'We used to be well paid for meeting our targets. Now the targets are given that cannot be met, so that they don't have to pay the bonus.'

Sri Lankan garment worker

Workers in every country studied reported extreme pressure to work harder, faster, and longer. An array of targets, incentives, and penalties are used to raise workers' productivity. Piece-rate pay – a fixed amount paid for each piece of clothing stitched, or each kilogram of grapes picked – is increasingly common. In Chile, one in three fruit pickers and packers paid by piece-rate earned the minimum wage or less. And they put in extraordinary hours to make it, facing an average workweek of 63 hours, sometimes up to 18 hours a day.[23] In the UK, manufacturers provide homeworkers with assembly kits that they say will take 14 hours to complete – but homeworkers report that they actually take 40. And they can legally be paid only 80 per cent of the minimum wage to do it. Under pressure from homeworkers' organisations, trade unions, and some high-street retailers, the UK government has at last committed itself to ending that legal exemption by April 2004.[24]

Kenyan garment workers commonly face penalties for lateness and mistakes, and charges for medical treatment. It can add up to more than a month's earnings. *'We've heard from many workers who have been charged and fined by their employers,'* said Steve Ouma, Senior Programme Officer at the Kenyan Human Rights Commission. *'Instead of getting a payslip at the end of the month, they got a bill – and it was deducted from next month's pay. It's outrageous that workers are forced to subsidise production this way.'*[25]

Long overtime at short notice

Overtime is voluntary by law, but for many women workers it is a condition of employment and imposed at short notice. In China, overtime is legally limited to 36 hours per month, but in Guangdong province the vast majority of workers surveyed across seven factories faced more than 150 extra hours each month.[26] One 'workers' handbook' in Shenzhen stipulated that 'When workers cannot do overtime they have to apply to the supervisors for a written exemption from overtime'.[27] Some factory managers compel workers to put in long hours by setting basic wages at a low level. *'I don't like doing overtime,'* said Seetha, sewing garments in Sri Lanka, *'but if I don't, then I won't have enough money. So we are forced to do overtime.'*[28] By law in most countries, overtime hours should be paid at a premium – but in reality, workers are often robbed of their rightful overtime earnings.

Overworked and underpaid

In order to raise output without raising costs, many employers use piece-rates, set excessive production targets, or falsify records of hours worked. For women workers it means long overtime that is hugely underpaid.

Morocco

Women in one Tangier garment factory put in around 90 hours of overtime in July 2003. But according to their employer, the extra hours were simply part of the workers' obligation to meet their targets, so did not count as official overtime. At the end of the month the women received only 50 to 60 per cent of their rightful earnings as a result.[29]

USA

Tomato pickers in Florida put in 148 hours of overtime work each month in the picking season. But since they are paid piece-rate, overtime pay doesn't exist. As a result, they earn between 50 and 80 per cent of what a long-term employee would earn for the same hours.[30]

Bangladesh

Garment workers from seven factories interviewed in 2003 worked on average 80 hours of overtime per month. Not one received a payslip. They were paid between 60 and 80 per cent of their due earnings – on average, the equivalent of doing 24 hours of unpaid work a month.[31]

Banned, bullied, and broke: troubles organising

'I used to think that the union was not important but after I got involved and met workers and unions in other factories, I realised how important it is to protect workers' rights. If a worker has a problem, they don't know what their rights are. The union can advise them and help solve it. I have gained lots of experience and now I know about the law. If I don't use it to help the workers, who will?'
Prem, a union committee member in a Thai factory producing for Banana Republic and Polo Ralph Lauren

In 2003, Prem's union succeeded in stopping the factory from hiring new workers on repeated provisional contracts and was seeking ways to support sub-contracted workers who are banned from joining the union by management.[32]

The freedom to join trade unions is fundamental for workers to improve their own working conditions. Unions represent their members on issues ranging from health and safety to salaries and working hours. They work both through formal 'collective bargaining' with employers and by assisting individual workers, for example, in cases of unfair dismissal or sexual harassment. They lobby national governments and international institutions to ensure that workers' concerns are reflected in national and global policy making. For decades, trade union struggles and solidarity have been central to securing and strengthening workers' rights worldwide.

'Here it is forbidden to create a trade union. Anyone in a union gets sacked.'

Esperanza, a garment worker in Honduras[33]

But unions face heavy restrictions, in law or practice, in many countries. Employers' tactics of intimidation, firing, and physical violence are exacerbated when governments fail to step in. And the transformations taking place in global labour markets pose an additional challenge. Traditional union members – male, long-term employees based in close-knit workforces – are rapidly being replaced and outnumbered by young, female, temporary workers in a migratory workforce with no history or culture of union involvement and little time to go to meetings. When the workforce is so fragmented, and if the legal employer's identity is blurred, the challenge to create a recognised, powerful voice for workers is huge.

Given the low incomes of their members, and the decline in their traditional member base, many unions do not have the resources to respond. Workers earning barely more than poverty wages may be reluctant to pay monthly dues, especially if they are often more afraid of losing their jobs than hopeful of winning better conditions. It creates a vicious circle: those workers most in need of collective support are the least likely to be recruited.

Raising women's participation is a key priority for many unions, but some still face barriers. *'The trade union helps us with many problems,'* said one South African fruit picker, *'and shop stewards show respect when we discuss problems with them.'* [34] But others workers were cynical, saying, *'Seasonal workers get very little or no opportunity to speak to the farmer. The union represents only permanent workers.'* [35] And in one Kenyan EPZ, women account for three out of four workers, but only one in five union representatives. Why? Union recruitment there often takes place in bars in the evening – places not considered appropriate for women. And issues of high importance to women, such as maternity leave and protection from sexual harassment, have not yet been raised in industrial-court disputes. [36]

Many unions are tackling these problems by joining forces with women workers' organisations, recruiting female organisers, setting up women's committees, and campaigning on women workers' concerns. By 1998, for example, more than two-thirds of the International Confederation of Free Trade Unions' national centres and more than half of affiliate unions were promoting the issue of women in leadership roles. They promoted action such as guaranteeing reserved and additional seats for women, and setting targets for gender balance. [37] And in the late 1990s, a network of its African affiliates launched initiatives to integrate gender perspectives throughout their member unions' work. [38] New national alliances are also forming. In Sri Lanka, for example, several trade unions and non-government organisations have recently joined forces as the Labour Rights Core Group, to campaign on critical issues facing women workers in the garment industry such as living wages, freedom of association, and compensation for impending job losses.

Sexual harassment

Many women interviewed said sexual harassment was a commonplace abuse of power in the workplace. Yet it often goes officially unreported, due to fear or a sense of futility. From Honduras and the USA to Morocco and Cambodia, women workers reported cases of male supervisors demanding sexual favours in return for getting or keeping jobs. Long shifts to meet deadlines put women's safety at risk. *'We are very afraid of being harassed or raped by gangsters, because we often have to work late at night and walk home in the dark,'* said one young worker in Cambodia. [39] Persistent harassment drives some women to leave their job, at the risk of not finding another. For Hasina, a former garment worker in Bangalore, India, the only alternative was to turn to sex work. *'You are subjected to all kinds of sexual harassment in the factory,'* she said. *'Supervisors, production managers, and watchmen touch you without giving you anything in return. In this job, at least you are paid for the same.'* [40]

Hidden costs beyond the workplace

Away from the factory floor and beyond the farm gate, precarious employment has long-term and community-wide costs. When women are employed without security and with minimal support from employers or the State, they bear the burden, often at the cost of their own health or their families' future, creating a long-term liability for society.

Children: the price paid by the next generation

'I don't want to get married while still working in the factory, because it makes our health poor and will affect our children's health too.' [42]

Cambodian garment worker

'We are here for production, not reproduction,' declared a Kenyan garment factory manager who refuses to provide paid maternity leave or childcare facilities. [41] This attitude may suit the short-term needs of his company. But when workers cannot care adequately for themselves or their children, the development prospects of the country are damaged.

Visit a garment workers' dormitory and you will occasionally see, pinned to the wall, a photograph of a small child. Nid, working in a garment factory in Bangkok, Thailand, has one of her son. He is two, and she left him with her parents in their village eight hours away, because there is no childcare provided at work. She sees him every three months, and is forced to take three days' unpaid leave for the journey there and back. [43]

Working women can be forced to consider extreme solutions to childcare problems. In one fruit-growing valley in British Columbia, Canada, one in three women fruit pickers – mostly Punjabi immigrants – take their young children with them to the farms, because of a lack of alternatives. [44] Even when childcare is available, arrangements can be extreme: one nursery school teacher in Colombia described flower workers dropping their children off at the nursery at four in the morning and picking them up at ten at night. [45]

School-aged children, too, often pay the price. Some working mothers can only cope with their double duties by taking their eldest daughters out of school to look after younger children, but the girls lose their chances of a more skilled job in the future. In Morocco, 80 per cent of women with older children had taken daughters under 14 out of school to do so – no wonder that many eventually follow their mothers into the factories. [46] School-going children are sometimes drawn into helping with their parents' work in order to meet production targets, even in rich countries. One school in the UK raised concerns that pupils who were children of homeworkers were neglecting their own homework (school work) in order to help their mothers meet their production targets. [47]

Long-term ill-health

Unhealthy working conditions mean that workers face medical costs, and their working lives may be cut short. Pesticide use on farms has an appalling history in some countries. A decade-long US medical study found that members of California's United Farm Workers organisation had elevated rates of leukemia and cancers associated with pesticide exposure.[48] A study conducted in a hospital in Rancagua, Chile, between January and September 1993 found that all 90 babies born with neural defects were children of temporary fruit workers.[49] Procedures have improved on some farms in the past decade, but in 2000, 62 per cent of female Chilean grape pickers surveyed reported being in contact with pesticides while working in the fields, while fewer than half of all agricultural workers there have occupational insurance coverage.[50]

Less dramatic but more common are low-level illnesses and injuries. Fruit and flower pickers and packers from Colombia, Chile, the USA, and South Africa commonly reported headaches, respiratory problems, and eye pain from handling pesticides. Garment factory workers from Bangladesh to Morocco commonly suffer headaches, coughing, vomiting, fever, and physical exhaustion. Poor ventilation in lint-filled rooms can lead to debilitating respiratory diseases. Hired in jobs that demand highly dexterous and repetitive movements, many women suffer joint injuries and back, leg, and shoulder pain.

Health and safety legislation may fail to prevent or recognise these illnesses specific to new industries and to women. Sri Lankan occupational health law recognises only gas-related respiratory diseases, not those caused by the fabric lint inhaled by thousands of garment workers, leaving those affected with no legal recourse.[51] US pesticide exposure standards are based on the adult male body, ignoring the higher risks for pregnant female agricultural workers, such as spontaneous abortion and structural birth defects.[52]

Workers often foot the bill for their workplace illnesses. *'When we get sick, we're the ones who have to pay the doctor,'* said Zineb, sewing clothes in Morocco for El Corte Inglés and other Spanish retailers. *'We don't have the right to get sick – they punish us if we do.'* [53] In Colombia, some women flower workers pay for health coverage that they never get. *'The employers deduct social security contributions,'* said one, *'but when we go to the doctor, they say that the employer is not up to date or that we don't even appear in the system.'* [54] Rokeya, a Bangladeshi garment factory worker, was ill at work for two months before she missed a day to go to the doctor. Her manager then deducted two days' pay, and she lost her full attendance bonus. On return she was told to work an extra eight hours unpaid to catch up with her target. In total, being unwell cost her 11 days' wages.[55]

'Sometimes you come home and you shake a lot and you cough and spit all night.'

Geraldine, picking tomatoes in the USA for Taco Bell

Challenges in the home

When women start contributing to household income, the household balance of power may be challenged, particularly with male relatives.[56] Some women find their status in the household improves. *'My family treat me better than before,'* said one young Cambodian woman now employed in the garment industry. *'I used to be scolded or beaten, but not any more, because now the family miss me and receive the money I send home.'*[57] Some women are able to play a bigger role in decision making and decide how to use their own earnings – but others face serious drawbacks. Earning an income can result in less financial support from other household members, especially from the fathers of the women's children, leaving them no better off overall and more dependent on keeping their jobs.[58] Women's employment may provoke violence from husbands and male relatives, who themselves may be out of work. In Bangladesh, garment workers reported facing threats and suspicion from their husbands when they arrived home at two in the morning, especially when their employers – hiding evidence of excessive overtime – had punched their official hour cards to show that they left the factory at six in the evening.[59]

Little change in caring work

'I am a woman worker, a housewife, a father, a mother.'

Maria, a Honduran garment worker.

When employed in short-term and unstable jobs, women are not in a strong position to re-negotiate their care-giving responsibilities at home. As a result, most continue to be the primary carers, with little or no support from their partners. In Colombia, women working long hours on flower farms are still expected to do almost all the housework: they report their husbands helping with less than 10 per cent of the time taken in childcare, less than five per cent of cooking, and one per cent of cleaning.[60] Likewise, in Bangladesh, women garment workers are still four times more likely than their husbands to be responsible for looking after sick children and dependants.[61]

Lose a community – gain a new, but transient, one

When women migrate for work, they often lose their ties with their traditional communities which had provided support such as childcare, informal credit, and neighbourhood security. As migrants, many face language and social barriers. In Cambodia the social stigma attached to young single women who have lived outside family control makes life difficult for them, even on brief visits home. *'Garment workers are not considered good women for marriage,'* explained one. *'In some cases engagements were broken off because the woman was a garment worker.'*[62] Likewise, flick through the pages of a Sri Lankan newspaper and you will see marriage advertisements that say *'Garment women, please do not reply.'*[63]

The loss of traditional support systems and poor prospects for marriage on returning home make women workers more dependent on new networks with fellow workers – a fragile dependency, given that their jobs are transient and unstable. Angela, sewing garments in a Kenyan factory, expressed frustration at her isolation from the wider community: *'It is not possible to do anything else. There is no time to take care of your own children, visit people, do business or go to college. Even going to church has become a problem ... We are somehow isolated.'* [64]

Trading away workers' rights

These harsh realities experienced by women workers provide eloquent testimony of a model of globalisation that is failing poor people. Over the past 20 years, while investors' rights have been deepened and extended through international trade agreements, workers' rights have moved in the opposite direction. In the absence of global institutions that are widely trusted and empowered to underpin these rights in the global economy, many governments have been trading them away. In law and in practice, they have eroded employment security, benefits, and protections in order to provide the flexibility demanded in global supply chains. But the short-term gains of this strategy can come at the cost of a long-term liability for society – and women workers are paying the heaviest price.

Ami Vitale/OXFAM

Six-year-old Kenyatta waits outside his home, not knowing when his mother will return from her job in one of Nairobi's garment factories. She is frequently made to work two extra hours of overtime, unpaid, in order to meet the day's production targets and finally gets home after dark.

2

Squeezed down the supply chain

Toby Adamson/OXFAM

In Chile's fruit packhouses, one third of workers earns only the minimum wage or less. In the fields, seasonal fruit pickers often work more than 10 hours a day, seven days a week, and the majority have no written contract. By law, seasonal workers are prohibited from bargaining collectively to improve their employment terms and conditions.

2 Squeezed down the supply chain

Who determines working conditions? There is, at one level, an obvious answer: the producers who employ workers – farm and factory owners and managers, because they are the ones who decide how to employ, treat, and pay their workers. One flower farm issues all employees with contracts, the next none at all. One garment factory negotiates with the workers' union, another threatens its members. One pregnant woman worker gets paid maternity leave, another gets fired. Why is it that some workers are empowered through their jobs, while others face precarious employment – and what can make the difference?

The vision of individual employers can make a difference. In every country, there are business owners and managers who are determined to respect the rights of their employees in the course of running a business – and they know that it can reward them too. *'Ten years ago, we invested heavily in our workforce, building housing, providing crèches. Then we set up provident funds and built health clinics on the farms,'* said one South African apple farmer. *'We were paying above the minimum wage to all our workers long before the law was introduced – it means higher productivity and greater loyalty, workers taking ownership of what they are doing. If you don't pay people enough and pocket all the profits, I'd say you are just stealing from them. To do this stuff is not cheap – other farms will always be able to supply cheaper. But it's the productivity of our people and management that pulls us through – that is how we keep ahead. It's our philosophy and we're sticking to it.'*[1]

Production management can make a difference too. Improving factory layout, planning, and personnel management can raise productivity and reduce pressure on overtime. And that can create a virtuous circle: when employees are well-trained and work reasonable hours, they tend to have higher morale, better quality levels, lower accident rates, and lower turnover – all adding back to higher productivity.

But two overarching factors influence the way that many producers hire and treat their workers:

- retailer and brand strategies in the supply chains
- government strategies on labour laws and practices

Together, the interaction of these strategies strongly shapes international trade practices and pressures and so can determine whether or not a job in a global supply chain is a way out of poverty for women workers. This chapter sets out a broad framework for understanding how trade shapes these two factors. Specific cases are examined: for the garments industry in chapter 3 and for fresh produce in chapter 4.

The rise of global sourcing companies

Over the past twenty years, trade liberalisation and communication innovations have dramatically increased the opportunities for retailers and brands to buy their products from producers worldwide.

- **Tariff reductions:** between 1980 and 1998, average tariffs on manufactured products fell from 10 per cent to 5 per cent in industrial countries and from around 25 per cent to 13 per cent in developing countries, cutting the cost of trade in goods.[2]

- **Foreign investment incentives:** export processing zones proliferated in the 1990s in developing countries, offering tax exemptions and investment allowances in order to attract local and foreign investors to produce goods for export.

- **Cheaper, real-time communications:** Internet-based software systems made real-time information exchange possible, and enabled just-in-time production and delivery coordination between producers and retailers on an international scale.

- **Cheaper transport:** with sea freight costs falling almost 70 per cent between the early 1980s and the mid-1990s,[3] and with significant growth in airfreight services, the delivery costs for distant producers have fallen dramatically.

The result is a new business model for major retailers, such as hypermarkets, supermarkets, and department stores, and brand owners such as leading clothing companies.[4] These retailers and brands have become 'global sourcing companies', outsourcing the production of the goods they sell to tiers of suppliers and producers through complex international networks, or 'global supply chains'. These supply chains are:

- **Driven by the big brands and retailers:** As gatekeepers to consumers, retailers and brands have tremendous power to determine price, quality, delivery, and labour conditions for suppliers and producers down the chain. Wal-Mart, the world's biggest retailer, buys products – including fresh foods and clothing – from 65,000 suppliers worldwide and sells to millions of households through 1,300 stores in 10 countries.[5] Such concentration of power at the point of sale creates huge leverage over producers. *'As things get more competitive, the pressure that comes along with that – yeah, we try to take advantage of it,'* said Gabe Meyers, a vice-president in global procurement.[6] No wonder Wal-Mart can sell at prices 14 per cent below its competitors.[7]

- **Segmented into high and low profit steps:** High-profit steps in the process – innovation, marketing, and retailing – are tightly guarded by retailers and brands. As Charlie Denson, President of Nike brand, explained, *'We have to keep renewing and refreshing what Nike stands for. The brand is the only thing we truly own, so we have to protect it.'*[8] In contrast, the low-profit steps – sourcing raw materials, production and assembly, finishing and packaging – are outsourced to mid-chain suppliers and low-cost producers worldwide.

There are serious power imbalances arising from the concentration of economic power in the hands of a few.

Report of the Panel of Eminent Experts on Ethics in Food and Agriculture, FAO 2000

- **Widely dispersed but tightly integrated:** Spanning continents, a supply chain can draw dozens of firms into the process of making and delivering a single product. Quality, technical standards, and logistics are closely controlled and coordinated. Li & Fung is a Hong Kong-based leading mid-chain garment supplier to major European and US retailers and brands, with US$4.8bn turnover and offices in almost 40 countries.[9] In making garments, the company may, for example, source fibre from Korea, dye and weave it in Taiwan, buy zips from China, and send it all to Thailand for assembly. *'This is a new type of value-added, a truly global product that has never been seen before,'* said company chairman Victor Fung. *'The brand tag says "Made in Thailand" but they're not Thai products. We dissect the manufacturing process and look for the best solution at each step ... and we're doing it globally.'*[10]

Global supply chains have created new opportunities for labour-intensive exports from low-cost locations. The result is a dramatic growth in the number of producers, heightening competition among the world's factories and farms for a place at the bottom of the chain. At the top end, however, market share has tended to consolidate among a few leading retailers and brand names.

Such an imbalance between intensely competing producers and relatively few buyers in the global marketplace gives retailers and brands the upper hand over their supply chains. Through the contracts that they negotiate and the conditions they demand, they can capture much of the gain generated by trade. The World Bank recognises this danger, warning that 'Local firms may not capture the benefit of the transfer of technology and increased productivity through networks if multinationals have a wide choice of production locations and a monopsonist position in the purchase of supplies [one buyer choosing among many producers]. In this situation, competition among suppliers may drive prices down, and the benefits of local firms' productivity improvements will accrue to the multinational.'[11] The same point was summed up by the owner of a Brazilian shoe factory, facing intense international competition to sell to leading footwear retailers in Europe: *'We don't sell, we get bought.'*[12]

Supply chain pressures create precarious employment

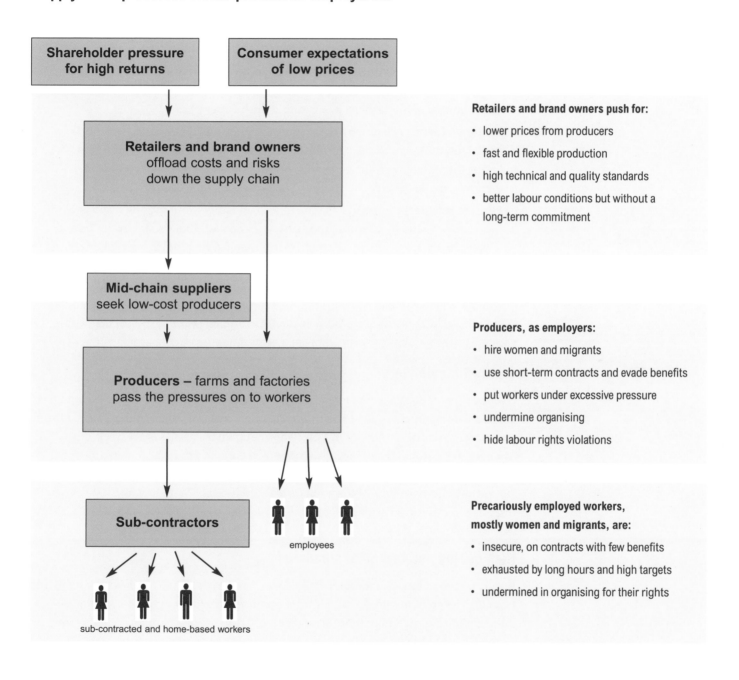

Shareholder pressure for high returns

Consumer expectations of low prices

Retailers and brand owners offload costs and risks down the supply chain

Mid-chain suppliers seek low-cost producers

Producers – farms and factories pass the pressures on to workers

Sub-contractors

employees

sub-contracted and home-based workers

Retailers and brand owners push for:

- lower prices from producers
- fast and flexible production
- high technical and quality standards
- better labour conditions but without a long-term commitment

Producers, as employers:

- hire women and migrants
- use short-term contracts and evade benefits
- put workers under excessive pressure
- undermine organising
- hide labour rights violations

Precariously employed workers, mostly women and migrants, are:

- insecure, on contracts with few benefits
- exhausted by long hours and high targets
- undermined in organising for their rights

Retailers and brands face three main sources of pressure which influence their supply chain strategies:

- **Shareholder expectations:** publicly quoted companies face intense pressure from their shareholders – especially major institutional investors such as pension funds and insurance firms – to deliver short-term returns in excess of 10 per cent on capital employed. Many companies deliver those results by stripping out low-profit activities and minimising the cash used in running the business.

- **Customer loyalty:** consumers have come to expect high quality and year-round availability at 'value' prices. Many retailers and brands compete to capture their loyalty through new products, short fashion cycles, and price wars, and so increase their own market share.

- **Ethical pressure:** unions, NGOs, concerned consumers, and socially responsible investors pressure high-profile companies to improve labour standards in their supply chains, through media exposure, campaigns, shareholder resolutions, and consumer pressure.

In an attempt to deal with all three, many retail and brand sourcing companies combine cutting-edge logistics with hefty bargaining power to push costs and risks down their supply chains.[13] Many have signed up to codes of conduct requiring compliance with labour standards down the chain – but when these interests clash, something has to give.

Just-in-time delivery

Electronic point-of-sale technology – that is, the barcode – has been increasing retailers' command over suppliers since the 1980s. Retailers no longer have to buy goods upfront and carry the risk of selling them. Now, when consumer purchases are tracked by barcodes, retailers can automatically reorder just enough products, just in time for restocking their shelves. It maximises their retail sales per square metre of shop space, and shifts order risks back onto suppliers and producers.[14] With this just-in-time response comes the pressure on producers to deliver smaller orders, in less time, and according to tightly planned shipping schedules – or face fines for delays.

High quality and technical standards

Retail and brand buyers demand reliable quality and high technical and safety standards from their suppliers, who demand it from producers. In the competition to supply, these criteria are becoming more stringent. To stay in the chain, producers must meet the standards of higher quality control, greater traceability, tighter control over hazardous inputs, and better record keeping – all at their own expense.

The buying game

Buyers working for retailers and brands operate in a business culture of performance targets and incentives which encourage them to squeeze suppliers on price and delivery times, with scant attention to the ethical repercussions down the supply chain.

High pressure to perform

Buyers are often given only 12 to 18 months to prove themselves before being moved onto a new product. '*You can try to negotiate but you don't want to upset them,*' said one South African grape farmer selling to several UK supermarkets. '*Every two years there's a new buyer, under pressure to perform – they must make margins and raise turnover, and they've got their ways and means of doing it.*'[15] It leaves little room for building long-term relations and understanding with producers.

Ethical standards: out of the picture

Buyers may get training or 'awareness raising' in ethical issues, but it is rarely integrated into the targets on which they are judged. According to one former fresh-food buyer at a leading UK supermarket, '*Buyers are caught in a high-pressure culture of weekly reporting on their sales and profit margin targets. Ethical trade just doesn't fit neatly into numbers and so it gets left out of the picture.*'[16]

Split personalities

Buying teams and ethical teams often sit in different company divisions, face conflicting performance targets, and put contradictory demands on producers. Producers are well aware of this disjointed approach. '*I know how to deal with the ethical code people from my many years' experience,*' said one factory manager in Shenzhen, China. '*I can judge the balance of power between buying departments and those responsible for codes of conduct to see where the real power lies.*'[17]

Pushing down prices

Buyers employed by many retailers and brands are given strong incentives to cut the prices they pay. Some use Internet 'reverse auctions', pitching suppliers into intense competition. Others demand 'open book costing' that requires suppliers and producers to reveal their production and delivery costs so that retailers can cut out low-value steps, and capture the saving in lower prices. Some boost their profits by charging suppliers for product promotions, for store displays, for discounts on poorly selling goods, for discounts on well-selling goods, and even for simply being listed as a supplier.

Short-term commitments

In search of ever-lower costs, better quality, and faster delivery, many retailers and brands, or their mid-chain suppliers, are ready to switch between producers for a better deal. This 'grazing', or 'churn' in the supply chain, keeps competition high and prices low, but leaves producers in uncertainty. Contracts with producers are sometimes verbal and easily broken if a better deal can be found; buying commitments often go no further than one season or just a few months.

Demands for better labour standards

Under pressure from unions and NGOs to improve labour conditions in their supply chains, many leading brands and retailers adopted 'codes of conduct' in the 1990s, with the best of those codes based on international labour standards. Some of these initiatives have helped achieve significant improvements, especially in health and safety conditions. But their approach is too often focused on ensuring compliance at the farm and factory level. What it fails to examine is the role of retailers' and brands' own purchasing practices – which demand faster turnaround, higher quality, and lower prices but without long-term commitment – in undermining the ability of farms and factories to meet labour standards at the same time.

International labour standards and codes of conduct

In 1998 the International Labour Organization produced the Declaration on Fundamental Principles and Rights at Work. In the declaration, the ILO's member states agreed that, regardless of their level of development, they should all respect, promote, and realise:

- freedom of association and the effective recognition of the right to collective bargaining;
- the elimination of all forms of forced or compulsory labour;
- the effective abolition of child labour;
- the elimination of discrimination in respect of employment and occupation.

Together, these are known as core labour standards.[18]

If corporate codes of conduct are to be useful tools for workers' rights, they must at least be based on these and other international labour standards, as set out by the ILO. A good code includes:[19]

- freedom of association and the right to collective bargaining are respected;
- employment is freely chosen;
- child labour is not used;
- no discrimination is practised;
- working conditions are safe and hygienic;
- living wages are paid;
- working hours are not excessive;
- regular employment is provided;
- no harsh or inhumane treatment is allowed.

Employers' strategies down the chain

Faced with intense pressures on cost, speed, and quality but without the commitment of a longer-term supply relationship, many producers down the chain lack the management training and tools to handle the pressures effectively – and they rarely get support from retailers and brands in doing so. Instead, they pass on the pressures through a mix of the following employment strategies:

- **Recruiting women and migrants:** women are typically perceived to be more careful, more compliant, and cheaper to hire than men. Migrant workers, with few alternatives to fall back on, often come from impoverished rural areas and so likewise can be paid less.

- **Hiring short-term:** employing workers on temporary contracts or through sub-contractors. For the employer, it cuts the cost of benefits, creates a workforce responsive to fluctuating orders, and discourages union membership.

- **Putting on the pressure:** setting wages, piece-rates, and production targets at levels that force workers to put in long hours at high speed to earn enough to live on – while enabling producers to meet tight delivery deadlines at low cost.

- **Undermining organising:** Intimidating unions, firing organisers, or harassing and abusing workers can undermine workers' efforts to organise and claim their legal rights, so reducing the costs to employers of paying for their rightful benefits.

- **Looking good:** when pressured to meet labour standards, many producers comply only with the most visible ones. Some fake compliance by falsifying records, hiding their use of sub-contractors, and intimidating workers into saying the right thing.

As shown in chapters 3 and 4, these employment strategies are being played out time and again in the fields and factories, workshops and homes found at the end of many retailers' and brands' global supply chains.

Governments' strategies on labour laws and practices

Governments face a range of choices in how they ensure that their country gains from trade. They can raise competitiveness by raising productivity, quality, and delivery. That calls for policies that include promoting education, management and skills training, backward linkages into the economy, and improved transport, communications, and shipping procedures. But these cost money to the State – money that is not coming in when foreign investors are offered an array of tax exemptions and holidays. An apparently easier strategy, especially in labour-intensive sectors, is to raise competitiveness by cutting costs: making labour cheaper and more flexible. No need for investors to pay – nor for states, at least in the short term. The resulting costs of precarious employment fall particularly on women workers and their families – and create a potential long-term liability for society.

Under international conventions, all member states of the International Labour Organization (ILO) are obligated to respect core labour standards – including the right of all workers to join unions and bargain collectively with employers. And many countries have legislation that provides good benefits and protection for workers too. But in practice, many governments, both South and North, fail to respect and enforce both international conventions on core labour standards and their own national laws. Competing pressures – from trade agreements, from local and foreign investors, and from IMF and World Bank advice and conditions – have led too many governments to develop labour laws and practices that put the needs of companies before the rights of workers.

Trade agreements and labour laws

The International Labour Organization is the natural home of labour rights and provides a unique tripartite structure which brings together governments, unions, and employers. But 43 out of 177 member nations of the ILO have not yet ratified both Conventions 87 and 98, which assure workers freedom of association and the right to organise and bargain collectively. And many of those that have done so still systematically undermine workers' organisations in practice. The ILO's 1998 Declaration on Fundamental Principles and Rights at Work obliges all its members to respect and promote these rights. But naming, shaming, and providing technical assistance are its most commonly used tools.

How to prevent workers' rights from being eroded by the pressures of trade liberalisation has been one of the most contentious issues in the debates on globalisation. Some have proposed adding 'social clauses' into World Trade Organisation agreements that would oblige member governments to ensure respect for core labour standards or risk a complaint from a trading partner that could result in WTO-approved trade sanctions. But others – particularly developing-country governments – have opposed the idea, partly out of concern that such a tool could be misused for protectionism, given the current imbalance of power at the WTO. Lacking a global institution that is both trusted and empowered to defend workers' rights, the debate has been stuck in an impasse.

Many regional and bilateral trade agreements have been drawn up in recent years and are currently being negotiated between developed and developing countries. The proliferation of such agreements is great cause for concern, because on matters such as agriculture, intellectual property, and investment, they do not take development needs sufficiently into account. Moreover, these agreements can increase competitive pressures to weaken workers' rights, especially when labour standards differ across signatory countries.

Some regional agreements contain clauses obliging signatory governments to respect labour standards, but these vary in their strength and effectiveness. For example, NAFTA, the agreement between the USA, Mexico, and Canada, contains a clause on labour, but only in a side agreement, and only requires governments to enforce their own labour laws, instead of meeting internationally agreed standards. The proposed text for the Free Trade Area of the Americas provides even weaker protection, merely requiring countries to 'strive to ensure' that their existing labour laws are not relaxed in order to attract foreign investment. Likewise, labour clauses of varying strengths exist in bilateral trade agreements, such as those that the USA has drawn up with Chile and Jordan. And the USA and the EU sometimes attach labour conditions in granting trade preferences to developing countries: the USA, for example, increased quota access for Cambodian garments and textiles in 2000 in part as a result of that country's progress in implementing national labour laws and complying with international core labour standards.

Such clauses in regional, bilateral, and access agreements could potentially play a valuable role in protecting labour rights. But, as with the wider debate on social clauses, there is a need to be cautious if the negotiating power of the parties is highly unequal, and if one party is in a position to dictate terms to the others and extract concessions. Any labour standards provisions in such agreements must be judged on whether they are a serious attempt to improve working conditions and livelihoods of workers, or are there for protectionist purposes.

Investor pressure: foreign and local

The mobility of foreign investors leads some governments to attract them with a labour force whose costs and flexibility fit with the demands of global buyers. Sometimes those demands are explicit. The American Chamber of Commerce in China claimed, in its 2002 white paper, that the costs of labour in China were getting too high in relation to the rest of Asia, and that the government's requirements for investors to pay towards social protection were unreasonable, complaining that 'recent legislation requiring a minimum wage and benefits for part-time workers has also placed an additional cost burden on employers'.[20]

Domestic investors depend on staying cheap and flexible in order to keep a place in supply chains. When labour laws clash with the dictates of the global market, many blame the 'rigidities' of national laws, not the excessive 'flexibility' demanded by retailers' and brands' sourcing strategies. According to one Moroccan garment factory owner, *'Our struggle is with the government to be competitive with countries further east where salaries are much lower. I place a lot of importance on what clients tell me – I accept all their pressures.'*[21] Others like him can use their political influence through employers' associations or as part of national or provincial elites to make it happen. In Sri Lanka, for example, the government and the highly influential Federation of Apparel Manufacturers have drawn up a strategy – without involving unions – to make the labour law more flexible to cope with the phase-out of the Multi-Fibre Arrangement.

World Bank and IMF advice

Throughout the 1980s and 1990s, the IMF and the World Bank recommended and required, through loan conditionality, that governments make their labour laws more 'flexible'. At the same time, they failed to insist that workers be empowered to represent their own interests in this process through trade unions and collective bargaining. Both institutions pushed policies to increase the use of temporary contracts, reduce maternity and social security benefits, extend overtime, and cut minimum wages across countries. In stark contrast, the right to union organisation and collective bargaining was left aside: in 1999 James Wolfensohn, President of the World Bank, said that the institution did not support these rights, because it did not *get involved in national politics*.[22]

More recently, the World Bank has stated support for core labour standards, at least from its headquarters. Further, a 2002 World Bank study on the effects of unions and collective bargaining in the global economy found that on average workers who belong to trade unions earn higher wages, work fewer hours, receive more training, and have longer job tenure. It also found that labour markets are better protected against the economic shocks associated with globalisation and liberalisation where collective bargaining exists.[23] But according to the International Confederation of Free Trade Unions (ICFTU), 'In contrast to the worker-friendly statements at the global level, country-level Bank staff still routinely advise governments to, in effect, violate the core labour standards by making access to unionisation and collective bargaining more difficult.'[24]

In 2003 the World Bank's private-sector lending arm, the International Finance Corporation, committed to making respect for trade union organising and collective bargaining part of its lending conditions. The IFC approved more than US$5bn in new projects for developing countries that year – but it is still just a fraction of the World Bank's total lending portfolio into which the policy could be introduced.[25]

Ideological overdose

When the IMF and World Bank recommend 'labour market flexibility,' too often it is a euphemism for weakening labour laws. The following examples illustrate their systematic advice to governments on labour policies.

Facilitate 'flexible' contracts

In 2002, the World Bank in Mexico called for 'eliminating labour-related rigidities' including 'the current system of severance payments; collective bargaining and industry-binding contracts … restrictions to temporary, fixed-term, and apprenticeship contracts'.[26]

Limiting collective bargaining

In 2001, the IMF in Chile 'viewed favourably certain aspects of the [government's] proposal (such as reducing restrictions on work schedules and allowing part-time contracts …). However it expressed concern over other elements (such as allowing collective negotiations at the inter-firm level …) which would reduce labour market flexibility …' [27]

Increase overtime hours, cut overtime pay

In Colombia, the IMF Stand-by Arrangement, signed by the government in 2002, made new loans conditional on reforms, including labour reforms that 'should reduce labour costs by extending daytime working hours and reducing overtime charges and severance payments'.[28]

Reduce gender-sensitive benefits

The World Bank in Bangladesh in 1996 advised the government to 'avoid introducing new regulations that increase the cost of female workers and thereby discourage their employment, such as maternity leave policies and regulations against women's working at night. Women have had good access to formal sector jobs in garments, where regulations have been minimal.' [29]

For any single country, this advice from international financial institutions may seem necessary to stay competitive with other cheap and 'flexible' countries. But the advice to 'flexibilise' has been given systematically to many developing countries. The result? Countries are still in tough competition over labour costs, but all at lower levels of labour protection. Workers' rights are simply being traded away.

Governments' response: trading away workers' rights

In the face of these commercial and ideological pressures, many governments follow a double strategy: attracting investors with financial breaks, and attracting them with low-cost and flexible labour. Both approaches give too much away.

Export processing zones – industrial parks offering tax holidays, duty exemptions, and investment-allowance reductions – have been popular incentives to draw in foreign investors. In 1975 there were around 80 EPZs, spread across 25 countries. By 2002 the total exceeded 3,000 EPZs in 116 countries.[30] But according to both the World Bank and McKinsey, a leading business consultancy, these incentives rarely work. Instead, they set national and provincial governments bidding against each other, so reducing the gains from investment for them all.[31] Benefit-free, union-free, and flexible labour is also a popular incentive offered to investors. And governments can end up bidding against each other, giving away many of the gains from trade to be had for workers, and for long-term development.

Promoting flexibility

Many governments passed laws in the 1990s to encourage flexibility – such as the easier use of temporary contracts and sub-contracting, more flexible working hours, reduced severance pay, lower overtime payments, and easier contract termination.

Giving away too much

The World Bank has criticised governments on two fronts for offering financial incentives to foreign investors. What the Bank ignores is that both criticisms apply equally to offering flexible and benefit-free labour.

Ignoring hidden costs

According to the World Bank, financial incentives to attract investors are often excessive 'because benefits (a new manufacturing plant, jobs created) are visible, whereas costs are hidden (tax revenues are forgone), governments may offer too much.'[32] But, likewise, governments offering union-free workplaces and benefit-free contracts overlook the hidden costs of precarious employment that fall on workers and their families – and the long-term costs to the State of poor health and insecure communities.

Bidding wars where all workers lose out

The World Bank says 'The use of investment incentives by developing countries poses a possible international coordination problem. ... [T]he possibility of excessive "competition" among developing countries may increase the likelihood that the "winning" country will have given away far more than it receives.'[33] But at the same time, excessive competition through labour market flexibility increases the likelihood that 'winning' countries – and their workers – lose out on their fair share of the gains from trade.

In China, for example, since the 1980s most migrant workers get only one-year contracts, and migrants across provinces lose their right of residence if they lose their jobs. It works well for employers, but it makes migrant workers extremely vulnerable. According to the Shenzhen Labour Bureau, *'The major component of the labour service market is temporary workers. Their characteristic is that they are active and flexible in the market. They are assiduous, hardworking, easily manageable and economically productive ... If there is work, they come; if not, they go. This lessens the burden on enterprises, solves the problem of labour use and at the same time does not result in urban overpopulation.'*[34] In other countries, too, labour law reforms have led to more workers facing repeated short-term hiring, with fewer benefits and with less bargaining power to push for their rights at work.

Fewer rights for export sector workers

Workers employed in EPZs can be denied the protection of national laws on minimum wages, hiring and firing restrictions, and rights to unionise, bargain collectively, and strike. The ICFTU's 2003 survey of trade union rights documented at least 16 countries – including Bangladesh, South Korea, and Malaysia[35] – where workers in the EPZs had fewer rights in law than those outside. In rich countries, too, exclusions of workers in some low-skill import-competing sectors have persisted for decades: in the United States and parts of Canada, for example, agricultural workers are excluded from the labour rights protections covering almost all other workers in the country.

Overlooking violations

Rather than weaken labour laws, a far greater number of governments simply fail to enforce them. A tacit understanding is built with employers that certain labour violations will not be challenged. The ICFTU documented cases in at least 32 countries where governments failed to protect the rights of workers in export processing zones in 2002, from Kenya and the Philippines to Viet Nam and Dominican Republic.[36] The severe under-funding of labour inspectorates in most countries testifies to the governments' inability even to know what is happening in most workplaces. And the absence of a gender perspective in inspection routines means that many problems facing women workers are commonly not detected.

The result? Instead of ensuring fair and sustainable gains from trade for workers, many governments are trading away workers' rights in the hope of a place in global supply chains. Weaker laws and lax enforcement of the law give a strong signal to producers to keep pursuing their strategies of employing workers in precarious ways.

Together, the influence of retailer and brand sourcing strategies and the result of government trade-promotion strategies strongly shapes the employment choices made by producers, and are turning potentially empowering jobs into precarious jobs. Chapter 3 shows these dynamics for the garment industry, chapter 4 for fresh produce.

3

Clothing the world

In Cambodia, one young woman in five is employed in a garment factory, producing primarily for export to the USA and the EU. The industry generates valuable revenue, but garment workers are still not getting their fair share of the gains.

3 Clothing the world

'I would like the people who buy these clothes to know their real cost, in terms of the sacrifices we make to produce them.'

Marta, 34,
a former garment worker
in Honduras

The cut–make–trim stage of garment production – where cloth turns into clothes – is a highly labour-intensive industry. No invention can yet compete with the speed and dexterity of a worker, usually a woman, at a sewing machine. And since sewing machines are cheap and mobile, investors have, for decades, shifted their factories around the world in search of new low-cost, competitive locations, knowing they will find workers wherever they go.

Worldwide manufacturers face retailer and brand power

Clothing factories, once located near to designers and retailers in the USA and Europe, started opening up in East Asia in the 1960s and have since been established on every continent, now providing valuable exports in a wide range of countries. Today, at least 50 countries look to garments for export success, and thousands of manufacturers – both local owners and foreign investors – are vying for a place in big brands' and retailers' supply chains. Why in such diverse locations? A mix of four factors influences location:

- **Low cost:** investors want quality, speed, and flexibility at a low price, so they seek cheap labour – as long as it comes with a stable economy, reliable electricity and phone lines, efficient shipping services, and easy access to fabrics.

- **Proximity to customers:** speed from the factory to the store is a premium for high fashion clothing, so drawing production closer to consumers. In the 1990s, US buyers turned more to Mexico and Dominican Republic; European buyers started sourcing in Morocco and Romania.[1]

- **Government giveaways:** many governments attempt to draw foreign investors with tax holidays, investment allowances, and even a 'union-free' workforce, by setting up export processing zones.

- **Trade preferences:** shifting rich-country trade barriers keep garment investors on the move, in search of the latest tariff cuts. The African Growth and Opportunity Act (AGOA), giving sub-Saharan African exports duty- and tariff-free access to the USA, has drawn many Asian investors to set up garment factories in Kenya, Lesotho, and Swaziland.[2] For 30 years the USA, Canada, and much of Europe have used quotas under the Multi-Fibre Arrangement to limit imports from developing countries. If it is phased out on schedule by 2005, Bangladesh, Sri Lanka, Thailand, Cambodia, and others fear they will lose many jobs to China.

Garment exports from selected countries

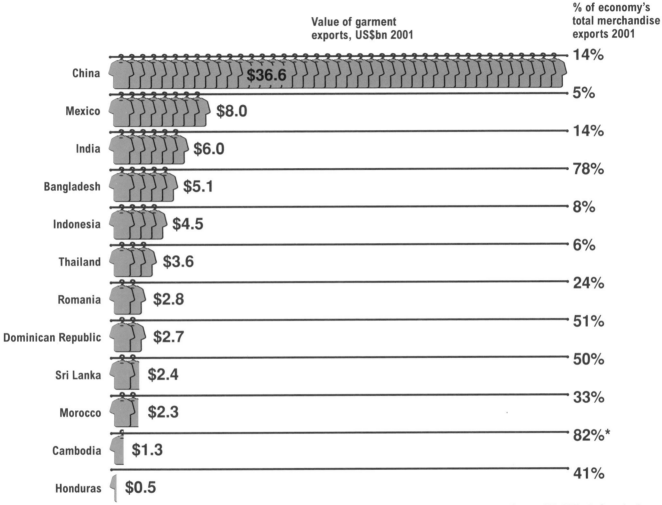

Value of garment
exports, US$bn 2001

% of economy's
total merchandise
exports 2001

Country	Value	%
China	$36.6	14%
Mexico	$8.0	5%
India	$6.0	14%
Bangladesh	$5.1	78%
Indonesia	$4.5	8%
Thailand	$3.6	6%
Romania	$2.8	24%
Dominican Republic	$2.7	51%
Sri Lanka	$2.4	50%
Morocco	$2.3	33%
Cambodia	$1.3	82%*
Honduras	$0.5	41%

Source: World Trade Organization
* 2002 data

The clothing industry is big business: the world's consumers spent around US$1 trillion buying clothes in 2000, with around one third of sales in Western Europe, one third in North America, and one quarter in Asia.[3] The biggest profits lie in branding and retailing. For brand companies, image and reputation are intangible assets, but they can be worth billions: in 2003 the value of Nike's brand alone was estimated at US$8.2bn, Gap's brand at US$7.7bn, and Levi's brand at US$3.3bn.[4] Multiple store retailers dominate clothing sales in rich countries: by the late 1990s, they had captured 70 per cent of the market in Western Europe and 85 per cent in the United States.[5] In 2001, the top five department stores in the USA – led by Sears Roebuck and JC Penney – controlled 56 per cent of department store sales.[6]

Hemmed in: pressure down the supply chain

Some retailers and brands use mid-chain suppliers to manage the production process, from fabric and component sourcing, design and product development, to identifying and negotiating with manufacturers, coordinating production, and logistics, packaging, and shipping services. Mid-chain suppliers can become multi-billion dollar multinationals in their own right, but are barely known by name. Other retailers and brands aim to strip out the costs of mid-chain agents by setting up their own regional offices, and sourcing direct from factories that take on more steps and upgrade to be 'full package' suppliers themselves. In either case, the focus is on speeding up production, cutting prices, and seeking locations offering ever-lower costs. Labour standards are usually far down the list of priorities – and workers bear the brunt of it.

The unknown giants in garment supply chains

Few shoppers have heard of Makalot, Li & Fung, or Esquel, but millions wear the clothes that they make for brands like Tommy Hilfiger, Abercrombie and Fitch, and Gap. These and other Asian multinational companies have low public profiles, but some are multi-billion dollar power-bases in the middle of garment supply chains. Many started out as manufacturers in Taiwan, Hong Kong, Singapore, and South Korea, then moved production overseas to cheaper locations. Now they specialise in coordinating production in their own and sub-contractors' factories, from Central America to Africa. Under pressure on price and speed, they often pass the pressure on to factories and workers down the chain. Unrecognised by consumers, and out of the eye of the media, they face little scrutiny.

Campaigning can make a difference to their practices. Taiwan-based Nien Hsing Textile Company is the world's biggest denim and jeans manufacturer and made profits of US$56m in 2002. Some of those profits came from its two factories in Lesotho, where 7,500 workers were making jeans for US and Canadian clients including Kmart, Sears, Gap, and Cherokee. Workers reported cases of repeat hiring on lower-paid 'casual' contracts year after year, unpaid benefits, verbal harassment, physical abuse, and dangerous conditions. Internationally, unions and NGOs in Europe, the USA, and Canada started drawing public attention to the case. In Lesotho, regional and local unions started an organising campaign to create a union for the two factories. The combined pressure led, in July 2002, to Nien Hsing committing itself to recognise and enter into collective bargaining with that union, once a majority of workers were recruited.[7]

Speeding it up

Retailers and brand owners are raising profits by cutting their costs and risks with 'just-in-time' ordering. They plan styles closer to, and even during, the fashion season, place smaller initial orders, reorder more frequently, and demand delivery just in time for selling in the shops. It reduces their exposure to fickle fashion trends, cuts down warehousing costs, and minimises the cash needed to operate – all good for raising shareholder value.

Two to four fashion 'seasons' each year was once an industry standard: now the norm is six to eight. At the leading edge, Spanish brand Zara can put together a clothing range in seven to 30 days and then replenish bestsellers in the stores in just five days. Specialty fashion retailers, like Zara and H&M, focus on faster-changing products at 'value' prices. *'The ability of these specialty [retail] chains to implement faster and more flexible supply chains is giving them a real competitive advantage,'* according to retail analyst Ira Kalish. *'These companies are particularly adept at understanding what consumers buy – and want to buy – in real time and responding quickly to sales trends and customer feedback.'* Their quick-response model puts pressure on traditional retailers and department stores to keep up.[8]

Quick response means shorter production lead times: from the day the order is received to the day that the garments must be shipped off to market. From Thailand and China to Honduras and Morocco, factory managers reported falling lead times. According to one Sri Lankan factory owner, *'Last year the deadlines were about 90 days ... [this year] the deadlines for delivery are about 60 days. Sometimes even 45 ... They have drastically come down.'* Promotions at Spain's leading department store, El Corte Inglés, drive shorter lead times in Morocco. *'Three years ago a standard order could take a month,'* explained one factory manager. *'These days there are some orders where the lorry arrives on a Tuesday, and on Saturday it's on its way back to Spain with the finished articles. This is because in Spain they have these "Fantastic Weeks" ... and the order is very urgent.'* That urgency turns into intense pressure for garment workers, as shown overleaf.

Poor planning by brands and retailers can further raise the pressure: some companies delay sending samples and make last-minute changes but still demand that production is completed on time, or place rush orders when shop supplies are running low. Factories that miss shipping deadlines can face hefty airfreight charges and lose their reputations; instead, they will go to extreme lengths – and work long hours – to deliver on time.

'Buyers pressure factories to deliver quality products with ever-shorter lead times. Most factories just don't have the tools and expertise to manage this effectively, so they put the squeeze on the workers. It's the only margin they have to play with.'

Rosey Hurst, director of Impactt, ethical supply chain consultancy

El Corte Inglés

Company information

El Corte Inglés controls more than 90 per cent of Spain's department stores,[9] with 110 stores in Spain, additional stores in Portugal, and total sales in 2002 of €11.9bn (US$14.2bn). Pre-tax profits have more than doubled since 1997, reaching €640m (US$762m) in 2002.[10] The company is privately owned; the president is Isidoro Álvarez.

Supply chain strategy

● Induyco, a garment sourcing company, works closely with the El Corte Inglés group. It supplied over 12bn items of clothing in 2001 from around the world.

● When sourcing in Morocco, Induyco sends fabric and accessories from Asia and Turkey to several locally owned factories in Tangier.

● For fast-moving fashion clothing, speed and just-in-time delivery are high priorities. Garments must be 'shop ready' when they leave the Moroccan factories, to minimise warehousing costs in Spain.

Ethical policy

There is no evidence that El Corte Inglés has a publicly stated code of conduct for labour standards in its supply chains.

Intermón

Spain

Morocco

Moroccan producers

At least 11 independent, small- to medium-sized factories in Tangier receive orders from Induyco for El Corte Inglés and other Spanish retailers. Together the factories employ more than 6,500 women, producing shirts, trousers, dresses, skirts, and children's clothes.

● *Falling prices* All factories interviewed reported falling prices, on average around 30 per cent over three years. '*Prices fall every year ... a pair of trousers worth €3.30 (US$3.90) three years ago is now worth €2 (US$2.40)*' said one factory manager. '*They always want higher quality garments, the price goes down due to competition and you're in no position to argue. At times the orders are extremely urgent and we accept them*'.

● *Production planning and lead times* In the last three years, lead times have fallen from 14 days to 5 or 7 days – some of the shortest in the industry.

'*The shops always need to be full of new designs. They (the buyers) give you an order today that should be ready in a week because they need to put it immediately in a department store ... We pull out all the stops to meet the deadlines ... Our image is on the line.*' factory production planning manager

Precarious employment for women workers

Most workers are single women, aged 20 to 30. One in three is illiterate. Many have no written contract; others are hired repeatedly on three-month contracts.

Excessive overtime

In high season, workers face 12–13 hour days, even up to 16 hours. By law, overtime must be paid 25 per cent extra. It is not. In one factory, workers faced around 90 hours of overtime in July. They should each have earned €300 (US$357). Instead they got €150–180 (US$179–214). *'Whenever I've asked why they don't pay us the 25 per cent extra for overtime hours … I created problems for myself which ended up with them sacking me.'*
Malika, 24

'We have a very young work force of women. We prefer hiring women because they are more disciplined. At times, the women have to stay up working all night and they understand perfectly the need for that flexibility.'
garment factory manager

Stress and health

Women reported exhaustion, backache, eyestrain, respiratory problems, burns, and needle injuries. In all factories, workers' use of toilets is restricted and monitored – kidney problems are common as a result.

'There's a girl who's seven months pregnant working 10 hours a day and as she has to make a lot of pieces per hour the employer doesn't let her go to the toilet. It's sheer torture for her, but she can't afford to lose her job.'
Khadija

Undermined in organising

Unions have faced twenty years of repression in Morocco.

'It is forbidden to talk about unions in the factories in Tangier. If they hear you talk about unions, they fire you.'
Fatiha, 25

Heavily underpaid

Young women aged 14–18 make up 10 to 20 per cent of the workforce in almost all factories, and they are paid only 55 per cent of the minimum wage. *'They pay as little as they can get away with,.'* said one, *'There is no work law here – the only thing that matters is that we work a lot in a short space of time. There are no rights.'*

Denied rightful benefits

In some factories, up to half of the workers are not declared to social security. Others cannot claim benefits through it.

'They deduct social security contributions from your payslip, but you don't know if the money will ever reach the social security department. If you go to check whether or not you are registered and then complain, they'll fire you.'
Saida

'When we are sick, we are the ones who have to pay the doctor. We don't have the right to be sick. One day when I was not well and I took a doctor's note to the employer, he gave me a written warning.'
Zakia, 36

Children's futures undermined

Lacking supervision and support, many children of the garment workers in these factories drop out of school early. Sons as young as 10 try to hitch into Spain on the undercarriages of trucks and tourist buses. Daughters start working in the garment industry as young as 13. Four out of five working mothers have a daughter who left school before 14 to look after siblings.[11]

Intermón

Moving on

The garment industry is in a state of constant flux, with mid-chain suppliers and sourcing companies ready to switch factories or countries for a small price cut. Such short-termism is greatly exacerbated by the impending phase-out of the Multi-Fibre Arrangement. *'In the textile sector, you live on a day by day basis, so we don't think too much beyond 2005,'* said one garment factory director in Cambodia.[12] In Indonesia, South Korean garment factory owners are likewise at the ready to move on. According to the Director of the Korean Trade Centre in Jakarta, *'The investors keep saying to me that the circumstances have gotten worse as they see labour movements rising ... They are eyeing China and Viet Nam as new locations.'* [13]But even within China, investors focus on short-term returns. *'I am a typical Hong Kong entrepreneur,'* said one factory director, currently in Shenzhen. *'Hong Kong businessmen won't invest huge money to wait for luck in the future. We've got no point to wait for returns beyond five years' time. Things change rapidly, especially in China, you know.'*[14]

Squeezing producers' margins

Growing global competition among producers is driving prices down. So too is the competition among retailers, who entice consumers with 'perpetual sales'. In the USA, for example, garment retail prices have lagged behind inflation since 1992 and have been falling since 1999.[15] The strategy is led by the high volume, low price retailers like Wal-Mart and Target, and their growing market share. By 2002, one in five US consumers bought most of their clothes from 'mass merchants' like these, and one in every eight garments came from Wal-Mart.[16] Retailers protect their profits by demanding lower prices from suppliers and adding on charges. 'Marketing contributions', for example, can be levied on suppliers to pay for shop display space or for a place in a catalogue; when profits drop, some retailers send buyers out to get 'profit contributions' from suppliers to boost them back up.

The combined effect is passed down to producers as falling prices, while production costs are rising for many. According to a manager of a Sri Lankan factory with good labour standards, *'Our wage and electricity costs have increased around twenty per cent over the past five years, yet the prices we receive have gone down by 35 per cent in the past eighteen months alone. I feel that prices are reaching rock bottom in Sri Lanka and I am not sure how we will survive.'*[17] In Honduras two factories producing T-shirts for export reported that the price paid per dozen had fallen from US$3.70 in 2000 to US$2.85 in 2003 – a 23 per cent drop in three years.[18] In China, too, average garment export prices fell 30 per cent between 1997 and 2002, while production costs rose 10 per cent from 1999 to 2002 – in part due to smaller and more varied orders.[19]

Wal-Mart worldwide: who pays for price cuts?

'Always low prices' promises the world's biggest retailer. With sales of US$245bn in 2002, Wal-Mart is number one in the USA, Canada, and Mexico, and making inroads into China, Brazil, and South Korea. Investors like the company: the share price has quadrupled since 1994.[20] Consumers like it too: in 2002 four out of five US households shopped there, and the company cut its prices for US customers by US$20bn. But producers and their employees worldwide bear the cost of those price cuts.

One US-owned factory in Kenya making jeans for Wal-Mart knows the pressure. Wal-Mart buys direct from the factory, but pushes down the price it pays by getting quotations from several global sourcing agents and challenging the factory to match the lowest price. In addition, Wal-Mart's buyers demand to know the price of every component and step involved in production, eliminating any profit margins on inputs.

Factory workers are left to face the squeeze. Excessive hourly production targets are almost impossible to reach. Few dare complain. Wal-Mart's own code of conduct is silent on trade union rights, but this factory has its own code. Rule Number Four: 'Every employee is entitled to freedom of association. You are free to join a trade union if you wish.' In April 2003, when they went on strike to demand decent pay, most union members were fired. Julia, a clerical worker, was rehired. '*Me, they gave me my job back. I was very lucky,*' she said, '*When I got there the management told me*

"*Next time, Julia, don't do that again. You did bad to join a union*" ... *Everybody wants the trade union, but they can't say it ... So we just keep quiet.*'[21]

Facing low profits and strict shipping deadlines, the factory manager sub-contracts orders out to another factory in Nairobi and pays that sub-contractor even less. No wonder that workers there face worse conditions. '*There are people working day, night, day, night without sleeping,*' said 33 year old Miriam, a sewing operator there, '*because they are told "You are not meeting the target, and the shipment is very near. And if the ship goes, we will transport these garments by air and it is very costly."*' Overtime is long and underpaid, sexual harassment is rife, and fear of being fired stifles complaint.

The Kenya Human Rights Commission, together with Workers' Rights Watch, a network of unions and NGOs, is campaigning for workers like these to be paid maternity leave, to receive a living wage, and to have the freedom to join trade unions. But targeting factory owners and managers alone cannot solve the problem. '*I hear that civil society considers the sourcing companies like Wal-Mart to be allies,*' said the director of one leading EPZ factory. '*You think that they can put pressure on us to improve the working conditions here. We should be putting pressure on them – for all they care, they want the products on time and at the correct price.*'[22]

Looking out for labour standards?

Quality, delivery, and price are key sourcing criteria – but what about labour standards? After ten years of initiatives in the garment sector, codes of conduct can be found posted on factory walls around the world. But workers' reports of insecure contracts, low wages and long overtime, extreme pressure, union busting, harassment, and extensive sub-contracting are still widespread. Why?

Far too few retailers and brands take labour standards seriously. Some have no published code of conduct, some others write their own codes but with weak standards and little effort to enforce them. A recent OECD survey of corporate codes of conduct found that out of 37 codes relating to the garment industry, fewer than half mention freedom of association, and two-thirds make no mention of monitoring systems.[23]

'I used to send workers to the hospital every week – they were suffering sheer exhaustion, fainting, losing their minds ... Sometimes I pass my former employees in the street – I dare not ask them about their health.'[31]

former garment factory owner, Thailand

Model codes based on international labour standards have been drawn up by companies, unions, and NGOs collaborating in multi-stakeholder initiatives such as the Ethical Trading Initiative in the UK,[24] Fair Wear Foundation in the Netherlands,[25] and Workers' Rights Consortium[26], the Fair Labour Association[27], and Social Accountability International[28] in the United States. Many leading retail and brand companies are members, and some have recruited ethical specialists and conducted multiple inspections. There have been some important improvements as a result, especially in the large factories that receive orders directly. Key changes commonly include: keeping more systematic records, paying minimum wages, reducing overtime, and implementing better environmental, health, and safety policies. *'After a while the auditors from the US came,'* said one Honduran factory manager, *'asking that we pay our employees better, that we improve the working conditions, that we pay and not discriminate. The investors are a key factor in all these processes in the industry.'* [29] Pressure from retailers and brands can clearly play an important role in improving working conditions – but there are still significant barriers to doing this.

First, many companies' inspections are too quick, fail to involve workers and credible local organisations, and focus on a checklist of health and safety standards. One Sri Lankan manager described the priorities of visiting inspectors. *'They are very particular about the toilets,'* he said. *'Recently they wanted the company to have a fire assembly point and to mark it clearly and to increase the lighting. Further they wanted the doors to open outward and not inward. The company had to renovate the building according to these recommendations and bear the cost.'* [30] Less visible problems – union restrictions, forced pregnancy testing, unpaid health benefits, and hidden homeworkers – are easily overlooked in such an approach.

Second, even good inspections cannot prevent all labour rights violations, because they only capture half the story. By focusing on problems at the point of production, factory inspections ignore the role of brands' and retailers' own purchasing practices in creating those problems. Excessive overtime is often the result of buyers demanding unrealistic delivery deadlines, then adding delays and sample changes at short notice. When retailers make no commitment to working with a factory, they undermine the manager's motivation to implement their code. *'I spent three years getting up to compliance with the SA8000 standard,'* said one factory owner in Thailand, *'and then the customer who had asked for it in the first place left and went to China.'*[32] When retail buyers face performance incentives focused only on making margins and keeping the store shelves stocked, they are unlikely to worry how such cheap and flexible production is achieved. *'The buyers are not too particular about the sub-contracting factories meeting compliance issues,'* said one Sri Lankan agent handling orders for Versace. *'We sometimes turn a blind eye too. We have to, or else we can't meet the deadlines or the low costs.'*[33]

End the double standards!

Five purchasing practices that undermine labour standards in garment supply chains:

- changing and delaying samples without extending shipping deadlines, often resulting in excessive overtime and sub-contracting;

- withdrawing when labour-standard violations are discovered, instead of working with the producer to become compliant;

- switching frequently between producers, undermining their commitments to long-term progress on labour standards;

- sourcing through agents and mid-chain suppliers who do not provide information on producers and workers down the chain;

- demanding improvements in labour conditions from producers without making the adjustments to price or delivery time required to make it possible.

Factory managers: passing it on to workers

'Most of the places I go all over the world, the contractor is not out of compliance because he wants to be or because he deliberately wants to cut corners. The problems with overtime, the problems with minimum wages or piece rate, the problems with harassment and abuse are because these factories are run on an incredibly crude basis. The retailers and the big brands are expecting very, very high levels of performance, and they keep raising the bar in terms of speed, cost, and quality. And what these contractors do when faced with that type of challenge is work harder rather than smarter.' [34]

Auret van Heerden, executive director at the Fair Labor Association

The world's best garment factories try to meet the challenge in smart ways: better management and planning and respect for workers' rights. In Sri Lanka and Bangladesh, for example, leading factories pay above-average wages on good contracts, achieve high productivity, and so require little or no overtime.[35] But these examples are the exception, not the norm. Most managers have no access to the management tools and training they need – and very few brands and retailers support them in getting it. Alternative responses to the challenge are more common: hiring women and migrants on insecure contracts, sub-contracting out, pressuring employees, undermining workers' organisations – and faking compliance with codes of conduct. Exacerbating the situation, many governments implicitly and explicitly reinforce these crude strategies by weakening labour laws and overlooking violations.

Hiring women and migrants on insecure contracts

Women make up 85 per cent of workers in Bangladesh's garment sector.

Women, usually young and often migrants, dominate in the cut–make–trim stage of garment production. In Kenya women make up 75 per cent of the factory workforce, in Sri Lanka 85 per cent. It reaches 90 per cent in Cambodia – where an astonishing one in five of all 18–25 year-old women in the country is employed in the garment industry.[36] Many are migrants from rural areas who have left behind their communities. Guangdong province, China's economic powerhouse, is a temporary home to 26 million migrant workers. Four out of five of those in the garment sector are women under 25. Since migrants across provincial boundaries lose their right of residence if they lose their job, they lose their bargaining power too: 60 per cent of those interviewed had no written contract, and 90 per cent no social insurance.[37] In Honduras, a growing trend among employers facing gaps between their orders is to send employees away without pay for any time between 15 days and six months, undermining their income security.[38]

Contract workers are sometimes brought in to expand the workforce temporarily without taking on employees. *'We use sub-contractors for Speedo,'* explained one Sri Lankan factory manager. *'The embroidery of the logo is done by workers to whom sub-contracting has been done ... We own the machines. The employees come under some other employer who looks after their welfare. We don't pay those employees. We only deal with their employers.'* [39] Sub-contracted workers face more precarious conditions and are less able to join unions. In one factory in Thailand, sub-contracted workers made up 10 per cent of the workforce. *'You can tell which ones they are,'* said Nok, a union member, *'because they wear a different uniform and they work on a different line. If they try to join the union and the factory owner finds out, he calls the sub-contractor and then the sub-contractor moves them to another factory.'* [40] Not surprisingly, these workers are rarely to be seen when labour inspectors visit.

Pay and productivity under pressure

Lacking the training and technology to raise productivity through better management and production methods, many factory managers simply pay workers low wages, set excessive targets, and demand long hours.

Workers in export processing zones are typically paid at least the minimum wage, but it is usually not nearly enough for a family to live on. Employers know it, and could raise productivity by raising wages but can face peer pressure not to do so. In Morocco, women workers are typically paid 8.5 *dirhams* (US 93 cents) per hour: the exact minimum wage. *'One of the bosses, who was a foreigner, wanted to pay 10* dirhams *[US$1.10] per hour and the [government] inspector told him no,'* explained an official at the Spanish Chambers of Commerce in Tangier. *'He told him to pay 8.5* dirhams *and that to do anything else would be dangerous because it wouldn't go down well with the other companies.'* [41]

Caught in the contradiction between buyers' demands for speed and low costs, and their codes requiring no excessive overtime, some managers simply increase hourly production targets. The impact on workers? Higher workloads for lower wages. *'Since no night work is allowed ... the hourly targets have increased dramatically and we have to work extra hard,'* said one young Sri Lankan woman. *'If night work were allowed, we would be paid overtime and the hourly targets would reduce too. That would be so much better than squeezing us.'* Problems with excessive overtime led the Sri Lankan government to raise the legal limit on overtime dramatically to 60 hours per month, far above the ILO's standard of 12 hours per week – so changing the labour law in order to accommodate the pressure of buyers' delivery deadlines. It still has not solved the underlying problem, because buyers' pressures have not changed. *'We try to restrict overtime to 60 hours a month,'* said the manager of one large factory. *'However sometimes we are forced to do much more.'* [42]

'When my child was sick I had to leave her for work, because if you didn't do overtime, they would dismiss you – it didn't matter whether it was day or night.'

Sophal,
a Cambodian garment worker

'Team 16 has reached 200 garments! They'll get their bonus!' bellows a supervisor down a microphone in a Moroccan factory. 'Come on team 12! You're falling behind!' [43] Many factories organise workers into teams with group targets. Workers report putting each other under extreme pressure to keep up, leading to exhaustion and repetitive stress injuries. Other factories resort to extremely crude methods of raising production, such as restricting access to the toilets. As one young woman in a large Sri Lankan EPZ company explained, *'We have a token system. For the entire line there are about 40 women and only two tokens. Workers have to compete among themselves to get the token. If we get caught using the toilet without the token, then we are given a warning and the bonus is reduced.'* [44] In an attempt to cope with these restrictions, many women skip meal breaks and drink as little water as possible – resulting in common cases of urinary tract and kidney infections.

Sub-contracting problems away

Brand and retail buyers looking for quality, reliability, and good labour conditions often place their orders with large factories that meet the standards. But these factories often sub-contract work out. Some, uncertain of future orders, take on too much work and cannot meet the deadlines alone; others sub-contract to cut costs; others still retain large orders for basic designs such as T-shirts, and sub-contract out the small orders for seasonal, varied styles, because they reduce productivity.[45]

'The TNCs [brands and retailers] don't allow us to do this,' admitted one Sri Lankan manager. *'However sometimes we are forced to in order to meet their deadlines. If a shipment of about 10,000 pieces is due, we do about 6,000 in the factory and give the rest to other factories who are willing to take it on.'* [46] The sub-contracting goes further: signs in the windows of neighbouring homes saying 'ironers wanted' give away the network of even cheaper homeworkers surrounding factory production. Time is saved, and money too: workers in Sri Lankan sub-contracted units earn 40 per cent less, without benefits, than those in formal factories; homeworkers often far less.[47]

In Morocco, too, sub-contracting cuts costs: a skirt made for US$3 in one large factory cost just US$1.80 from a sub-contractor. *'These workshops give us flexibility and also a good price level,'* said the factory manager. *'They produce at 30 per cent lower labour costs.'* [48] In Kenya, large orders from Wal-Mart placed with one EPZ factory are then sub-contracted out to several others. *'We are never sure of whether the next order will be coming,'* said one sub-contractor, *'You cannot therefore engage people on a regular basis when you are not sure that there will be work.'* As a result, he hires workers on a daily basis for months on end.[49]

Out of sight of buyers and inspectors, workers in sub-contracted units and homeworkers are caught in highly precarious employment and working conditions. In addition to lower pay, written contracts are rare, few workers are ever enrolled in social security schemes, and working conditions are cramped and often hazardous. In 2002, the closure of a large Thai company producing for international brands revealed an extensive network of sub-contracting and extremely harsh conditions for workers (see box below).

Undermining organising

Factory managers in many countries are threatened by the prospect of empowered workers. '*We do not at all encourage trade unions,*' explained one Sri Lankan employer producing for Gap and Wal-Mart. '*Rather we completely discourage them. Even though at one time the buyers demanded that we permit the setting up of trade unions, we refused. We don't see the need for trade unions. If there is a problem, the employees can report to the management.*'[50] The tactics for undermining unions are diverse, and governments can exacerbate the problem. In some countries, such as China, there are legal barriers to establishing representative and democratic trade unions. And many companies take advantage of it. '*As soon as a union is organised in a factory, management threatens to relocate to China or Viet Nam,*' said Reynaldo, a union organiser in export processing zones in the Philippines.[51]

Sub-contracted out of sight in Thailand

In August 2002, Bed and Bath Prestige, a Thai garment manufacturing company, was receiving orders for Levi's, Nike, Adidas, Harley Davidson, and many American universities. Then it closed down overnight, leaving its 900 workers with no severance pay and owed millions of *baht* in wages. Many of the former workers organised to fight for their rights and, in doing so, pieced together what they knew about the company's operations, revealing an extensive network of sub-contracting.

Orders had been accepted far in excess of the factory's capacity and sub-contracted out to workshops employing around 1,100 workers. Eight of those workshops were in Mae Sod, on the border with Burma, where four out of five workers were Burmese

migrants, many illegal. '*They were paid 40 to 50* baht *per day,*' recalled one former employee from Bed and Bath's official factory (that is, US$1–1.25, around 30 per cent of the minimum wage). '*And because the sub-contractors' shops are hidden inside or upstairs, outsiders could hardly know about their operations.*'

Out of sight and outside the law, these workers endure 12-hour days and intense harassment from the police. HIV/AIDS and abortions are both problems arising from the mixed dormitories and workers' lack of sex education. Pregnant women are fired, and the migrants' children, with no access to education, often fall into gangs and crime.[52]

Some employers refuse to recognise or negotiate with unions, violating the workers' right to collective bargaining. Committee members in several Thai garment factory unions reported that they would be the first to be laid off when orders fell, or would be continually excluded from overtime shifts, reduced to a basic wage too low to live off. Honduran garment workers say that a reputation for activism will follow them. *'If you apply to a new factory,'* explained one woman, *'the management gets in touch with your old employer to find out why you left. If it was because you were in the union, you'll get turned down.'*[53]

Faking it

Caught between intense production pressure and inspections of labour standards, some factories rely on fooling inspectors – and when visits are quick, announced in advance, and conducted by foreigners, it is relatively easy. Double book keeping hides the long hours. Gita, working in a leading Sri Lankan garment factory, each month receives a paper bag that has her pay slip printed on it – but with no mention of her overtime hours. Inside the bag, with her earnings, is another piece of paper.
She explained, *'This is the overtime pay. The company does not include overtime payment in the pay-slip itself, because then the people coming to the factory would know that we have been working more than the overtime hours allowed. We have been instructed by the company not to show this piece of paper when they come to question us.'*[54]

Coaching and bribing workers is common. One pregnant Thai worker described the instructions from the personnel manager before an inspection. *'He said the customer will ask "Do you work overtime?" and we have to say "No!"' But in reality pregnant workers work overtime and on Sunday as well. We sometimes work until two in the morning or till dawn, but we have to say that we work overtime only until eight in the evening ... If we lie, we will get paid 400 baht [two days' wages].'* In China, several factory managers admitted to using an array of tools for passing the compliance test, despite extreme violations of the code's standards (see table opposite).

Governments can make it easy for factories to get away with poor labour standards. In Kenya, labour inspectors did not have the right to enter export processing zones until mid-2003. The government of Bangladesh, under pressure to introduce reforms in order to retain US trade preferences, and aiming to build a good reputation for labour standards, has committed itself to lifting its ban on trade union activities in EPZs by January 2004. Fierce competition in China for foreign investment between provinces can leave law enforcement a low priority. *'The labour regulations simply are not working here – nobody cares to enforce them, not even the trade union or the labour bureau,'* said one company director in Shenzhen, China.[55]

In many countries, labour inspectors are too few or paid too little to ensure that workers' rights are enforced. In Thailand in 2002, there were just 600 inspectors visiting 300,000 factories – that is one inspector for every 500 factories.[56] In Bangladesh, there is a backlog of 10,000 workers' cases waiting for a hearing at the labour courts, and each can take four to five years to settle.[57] In Morocco, inspectors are paid US$238 per month – just above the minimum wage – leaving them open to corruption. *'The labour inspection means nothing,'* said one women workers' organiser. *'When the inspector visits the company, he meets with management. He has a coffee with the personnel boss, goes into the control room, chooses a suit, tries it on and off he goes.'* And in Bangalore, India's fashion garment hub, one labour inspector admitted, *'We have received instructions from above to be lenient in inspections as these factories are contributing to the economic growth of the State.'* [58]

Faking it: how to pass inspections in Guangdong province, China

Retailers and brands sourcing from the factory	Monthly overtime hours (legal limit 36)	Workers' experiences	% not receiving minimum wages according to hours worked	Employment status and rights	Management methods of deceiving inspectors and visitors
Factory A: Wal-Mart Explorer No Boundaries	150–200	Overtime often runs past midnight, and workers have only one day off each month	35%	No maternity leave No social insurance coverage 60% have no contract Piece-rate pay with no overtime premium	False documents on wages and hours Coaching workers to answer questions
Factory B: Toys R Us First Impressions Wal-Mart	180–250	Workers are fined for being late, answering back to managers, and not making their beds	50%	No written contracts No maternity leave No social insurance coverage Piece-rate pay with no overtime premium	Double sets of workers' punch cards Coaching workers to answer questions Dismissing uncooperative workers
Factory C: Target Sears Tommy Hilfiger	80–180	Two to three women suffer head injuries each week after passing out from exhaustion	40%	Two or three times a month the workers have to work all night. But there is no overtime, only the basic piece-rate pay	False documents on hours and wages Broadcasting training to workers on how to answer questions Threatening workers

Source: Liu, K.M. (2003)

Paul Weinberg/OXFAM

4
Injustice in the fields

On South Africa's fruit farms, women get the seasonal and temporary jobs,
year after year. Working up to 11 hours a day at harvest time,
the vast majority earn only the minimum wage with no paid leave,
no maternity leave, and no security of employment.

4 Injustice in the fields

Green beans and baby sweetcorn from Zambia and Kenya; fresh flowers from Colombia, Holland, or Ecuador; apples, grapes, and wine from South Africa, New Zealand, or Chile – supermarket shoppers have never had so much low-cost choice and world-wide variety delivered to their shopping baskets. But Oxfam's research with partners in South Africa, Chile, the United States, and Colombia has found that, across different national contexts, supermarkets and food industry buyers are capturing the lion's share of gains from this trade, while passing risks and costs on to farmers. And many farmers pass them on too, as precarious employment for the women who pick and pack their fruit and flowers.

Worldwide growers facing supermarket superpowers

In search of an escape from falling commodity prices, many countries have been turning away from maize, sugar, and coffee and towards higher-value exports like fruit, flowers, and wine. The shift has been strongly encouraged by lower tariff barriers, rising consumer demand for year-round fresh food, and better technology that makes long-distance transport and storage possible and affordable.

The result is that high-value and processed foods now account for two-thirds of all agricultural trade and provide valuable export revenues and employment for many countries.[1]

- Colombia's cut flowers have surpassed coffee in export earnings and are second only to Holland's in the volume traded. In 2000, the sector generated US$580 million in export earnings and employed 80,000 workers.[2]

- Exports of Chilean fruit more than doubled from 1982 to 1992, reaching US$1bn by 2000 and providing six per cent of the country's total export earnings.[3]

- In South Africa's Western Cape, 50 to 85 per cent of deciduous fruit (such as apples, pears, plums) is exported, with the sector contributing 20 per cent to the province's agricultural output and employing more than 75,000 workers.[4]

- US exports of fruits, vegetables, flowers, wine, and other labour-intensive horticultural products grew from US$4.5bn in 1989 to US$11.3bn in 2002, employing 1.6m farm workers.[5]

Intensely competing producers

Competition to export fresh produce has grown dramatically over the past twenty years. Colombia pioneered cut-flower exports from the South in the 1970s; Ecuador, Kenya, and others later followed, and by 1999 Southern exports held 30 per cent of the global market.[6] Global apple production is expected to grow more than 20 per cent between 1998 and 2005, with big export increases from China, Europe, and South America.[7]

Since 1994, NAFTA has intensified competition; for example, between tomato growers in Mexico and Florida,[8] and between strawberry growers in the USA and Canada.[9]

Countries are competing harder – so too are companies. Since the late 1980s agricultural marketing boards in many countries have been replaced by many individual exporters. Such a shift typically raises efficiency and product quality, but it can also erode farmers' leverage with overseas buyers. When South Africa's deciduous fruit marketing board, Unifruco, was dismantled in 1994, fruit farmers as a group lost much of their bargaining power. Importers and international traders were no longer negotiating with a handful of large national exporters, but with a multitude of small and medium-sized, resource-poor local firms.[10]

Food retailers: global superpowers

Over the past twenty years, fresh produce in retail and food service industries has headed in the opposite direction: towards global consolidation. In the food service industry, US-based Yum Brands has 33,000 restaurants – including Taco Bell, Pizza Hut, and KFC – in over 100 countries, and is especially focusing on expansion in China, Mexico, and South Korea.[11] Supermarkets – grocery retailers with multiple stores – dominate food sales in rich countries and are rapidly expanding their global presence.

- In the USA, supermarkets and even bigger 'supercentres' owned by companies like Wal-Mart and Kroger controlled 92 per cent of fresh-produce retailing by 1997.[12] In the UK, just five supermarket chains controlled 70 per cent of the market by 2003.[13]

- Supermarkets now control 55 per cent of all food retailing in South Africa,[14] 50 per cent of fresh-produce retailing in Brazil, and 30 per cent in Argentina and Mexico.[15]

The world's top food retailers

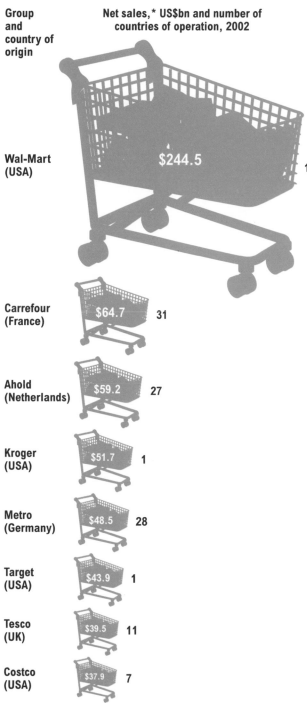

Group and country of origin	Net sales,* US$bn and number of countries of operation, 2002
Wal-Mart (USA)	$244.5 — 12
Carrefour (France)	$64.7 — 31
Ahold (Netherlands)	$59.2 — 27
Kroger (USA)	$51.7 — 1
Metro (Germany)	$48.5 — 28
Target (USA)	$43.9 — 1
Tesco (UK)	$39.5 — 11
Costco (USA)	$37.9 — 7

Source: www.planetretail.net Top 30 Grocery Retailers Worldwide
*Net sales include non-grocery goods

- In Europe, Carrefour of France and Metro of Germany now make almost half their revenue from sales overseas – for Holland's Ahold, it is 85 per cent.[16]
- In China, Wal-Mart had 22 stores by 2001; Metro had 15, and Carrefour had 28 hypermarkets. In Thailand in 2003, Tesco had 48 stores; Carrefour had 19 in joint ventures, and Ahold, likewise, had 55.[17]

Freshly squeezed: pressures down the supply chain

Fresh produce is a high priority for food retailers. Placed at the front of the store, fruit and vegetables are displayed to attract new customers and to signal quality and value. They are good for profits too, typically providing retailers with 30 to 40 per cent gross profit margins – among the highest in the business.

Some supermarkets are shortening their fresh-produce supply chains by forging closer links to farms and plantations. Many have created a core of first-tier suppliers responsible for sourcing, ordering, importing, and delivering, say, the carrots or apples or mangoes needed by the supermarket. In the extreme, Wal-Mart (Asda in the UK) nominates just one supplier for each category, in a mutually exclusive deal. Most other supermarkets divide each category among two to four suppliers, giving each 30 to 40 per cent of the business. These first-tier suppliers then set 'programmes' through exporters with domestic and overseas farmers, specifying the quantity and quality (but often not the price) of the produce required through the year. They are under tremendous pressure to deliver low-cost, high-quality fruit, week in, week out, just in time for putting onto the shelves.

'We employ people as we need them, but you need to break their expectation of having a permanent position, so you hire for two to three weeks and then you let them off for a few weeks, and then you hire them again.'[18]

South African apple farmer

Since supermarkets are increasingly controlling food retailing, the world's farmers are competing for a place in their supply chains. It can be good business, especially for farmers selling top-quality and out-of-season produce. If they can meet the high standards (not easy, given the uncertainties of weather, pests, and long-distance transport), then they get the big benefit of a sure sale over the coming season. But fresh produce is a risky business. And the extreme imbalance in negotiating power between a handful of supermarkets and the world's farmers means that most of the gains from trade are captured at the top. Supermarkets are pushing price and payment risks onto farmers and growers, controlling packaging and delivery requirements, squeezing producers' margins, and focusing on technical, not ethical standards.

Exporting apples from South Africa to UK supermarkets

Each actor in the supply chain adds to the retail price for apples to cover costs and margins

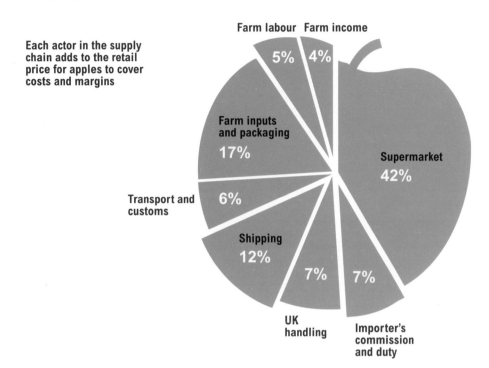

Farm labour 5%

Farm income 4%

Farm inputs and packaging 17%

Transport and customs 6%

Shipping 12%

UK handling 7%

Importer's commission and duty 7%

Supermarket 42%

Source: 2003 data based on information from Deciduous Fruit Producers Trust and various exporters and importers.[19]

Raising risk

Some supermarkets push for exclusive agreements with growers and exporters. *'The English are very annoying,'* said one Chilean fruit exporter supplying Asda and Tesco. *'They are interested exclusively in their own business, they do not want me to sell to another supermarket ... If I want to, I am told, "Well, stay with them then."'*[20] The benefit that supermarkets offer is assured sales through 'programmes' – but these are not binding. Agreements are often verbal, so there is no written contract to break. *'Only a very small portion of the fruit is traded under a signed, legally binding contract,'* explained another. *'It can sound incredible, but it is that informal.'*[21] Such informality gives buyers flexibility to delay payments, break programmes, or cancel orders, forcing suppliers to find last-minute alternatives. *'They chop and change their minds constantly,'* according to an apple packhouse manager in South Africa. *'It takes one month for us to get the fruit there, but it takes two minutes for them to change their minds ... then the only thing we can do is dump it somewhere else.'* Wine producers face this uncertainty too. *'We are penalised if the product is not delivered on time – but if the retailers decide they don't want it, it's up to the producer to sell it elsewhere.'*[22]

Exporting flowers is a sophisticated business in Colombia, but it is conducted on incredibly informal terms. *'Years ago when I'd get an order by phone from the States, I'd say, first you send me the money, then I'll send the flowers,'* explained one producer. *'Today, I have to send the flowers first and they pay 60 days later ... If I ask for a letter of credit, the buyer just says, oh let's not worry about that – there are plenty of others who will send me flowers without one.'* [23]

Farmers carry the risk of volatile prices too. The volume of fruit to be shipped to the supermarket is agreed in a programme, but often the price is not. Supermarkets fix the margins they want and leave suppliers and farmers to bear any price fluctuations. *'The supermarkets are looking for a 30 per cent margin and say they want to sell grapes at 99 pence (US$1.70),'* explained one South African grape farmer. *'So they tell the importer that he must underwrite the deal: if he can't supply them with grapes at 66 pence (US$1.13) for the season, he must write them a cheque for the difference.'* [24]

Even though exporters and importers stand in the middle, they usually operate as agents on a commission, leaving the farmer with the price risk. A Chilean grape exporter explained, *'I try to get the best profit for their fruit ... I deduct eight per cent for my fees, and I also deduct costs for materials and transport services – and what's left is for them.'* [25] That means farmers carry the cost if the fruit is rejected on arrival, if supermarket buyers find a cheaper source, or if the buyers run low-price promotions to capture market share from other supermarkets. *'I talked to my financial manager the other day,'* said one apple farmer in South Africa, *'and he said, "When you deliver your fruit, who do you invoice?" I said no one and that I wait for the price to be told to me. He said, "You're not farming, you're gambling."'* [26]

Commanding control

Product standards, such as those set by the European Union, can be highly specific, raising fertiliser costs and reducing yields. *'Now they are telling us that the size of a Fuji apple is ideally 65mm, not 63mm,'* explained a South African apple farmer, *'so when you are thinning you have to tell the workers to cut more deeply ... There is more skill involved, but it also takes longer and there is more labour.'* [27] At the packhouse, individual supermarkets – especially in the UK – require the fruit to be packed using their own bags, crates, and sizes, increasing the complexity of the work. *'The worst thing for us is the additional requirements that retailers give us,'* said a South African packhouse manager. *'Now they want the fruit packed in a plastic tray, and that becomes expensive ... they want another kind of pallet, a chipboard pallet. Those things cost us.'* [28]

Delivery schedules for fresh produce are extremely tight. Cut flowers and baby vegetables are airfreighted from Kenya and Zambia to the UK, with supermarkets placing their orders for produce to be sent the same day. For the supermarkets, it means tight control over well-stocked shelves, but for women workers, same-day orders mean long and unforeseen overtime. Likewise, fruit transported by ship can spend two weeks at sea, but packhouses must still meet tight deadlines to ship orders in time. Add to that increasingly complex and supermarket-specific packaging, and the result for women employed in packhouses is long hours of working at high speed to deliver on time.

Squeezing producers' margins

While producers have faced rising costs of higher product and quality standards, the real prices paid to producers for many products have been stagnant or falling. Real export prices paid for South African apples have fallen 33 per cent since 1994.[29] Florida tomato growers have seen the real price paid for their tomatoes fall by 25 per cent since 1992 – unsurprising, given the growing consolidation among those producers and given the increasing competition with Mexican imports, but US supermarkets have raised the real price to consumers by 46 per cent at the same time.[30]

Supermarkets usually offer a marginally better price than wholesale markets – but they have other ways of clawing back costs. *'Buyers are using fresh produce as a stepping stone to something bigger,'* claimed one South African apple farmer. *'There's pressure to build markets and wring out greater margins. The buyers are there to build a reputation for themselves: it is the growth in market share.'*[31] Typically managing a product category for 12–18 months, produce buyers have to prove themselves fast and are judged, rewarded, and promoted on the overall profit they make – both by widening profit margins and by imposing an array of fees and charges.

Fees and charges are big business for supermarket buyers. A UK government enquiry into supermarkets in 2000 found that at least one third of their UK-based suppliers had faced the following demands: to pay a fee just to be listed as a supplier; pay another fee to get shelf space; change orders at short notice; be paid later than agreed; contribute to nominated charities; give a 'profit contribution' to boost the supermarket's own earnings; and pay for product promotions.[32] The government introduced a code of practice in 2002, regulating the relations between supermarkets and their suppliers, which is binding on the top five. But after one year in practice, many UK farmers and suppliers were cynical about the code's ability to make a difference to supermarket practices, and remain reluctant to bring complaints forward for fear of being de-listed.[33]

'Prices are negotiated with my hands tied behind my back, with a blindfold. They really screw you to the floor.'

South African wine producer selling to UK supermarkets

Setting standards? Technically strong, ethically weak

Codes of conduct are widely used in the fresh-produce industry. But they are heavily focused on technical, not ethical standards, aiming to ensure healthy and safe food for consumers, but not decent and secure jobs for workers.

European retailers, including Ahold, Migros, Metro, Tesco, and Asda, and their suppliers have jointly created EUREPGAP, a rigorous technical and environmental code for farmers to follow. 'Major' requirements include: product traceability to the farm level, the use of approved fertilisers, keeping detailed records of pesticide use, providing evidence of residue testing, and ensuring pest control in packhouses. Worker welfare has been left off the agenda, mentioned in just one line as a 'minor' requirement to comply with national labour laws.[34]

Taco Bell, owned by Yum Brands, has also set standards to be met by its producers – but only on animal welfare. *'Taco Bell has a policy that it will not buy food from contractors that mistreat animals,'* said Lucas Benitez, a leader of the Coalition for Immokalee Workers, representing Florida tomato pickers. *'All we are asking is that they have the same policy for humans.'*[35]

In Colombia, private inspectors visit the flower farms on behalf of the European companies that own the patents on the plant varieties grown, to check they are not being infringed. In contrast, the Colombian government has several times proposed to reduce the number and capacity of labour inspectors responsible for ensuring that workers' rights are not violated. Under pressure from NGOs and consumers, the flower exporters' association, Asocolflores, created its own code covering employment and environmental standards in 1996, but it falls short of recognising workers' rights to join trade unions and bargain collectively.[36]

Even codes focused on labour standards are not reaching those most needing their protection. An advanced initiative operates in the UK, where many supermarkets have adopted the Ethical Trading Initiative's model code. But some inspections only cover packhouses, and do not reach farm workers. It is in striking contrast to standards on farm-level traceability. *'If someone bought a slice of ham at a supermarket, took it home and became sick,'* explained one Chilean fruit exporter, *'the supermarkets would want to know what pig the ham came from, almost what the pig's name was ... That is what traceability means.'*

In contrast, however, supermarkets often claim that their supply chains are too complicated to find and inspect all the farms. And when farm inspections have taken place, too many are conducted quickly by using checklists, with no involvement of workers and inadequate attention to women's and temporary workers' concerns.

'People visit the farm, but it is a waste of time,' said a South African wine grape farmer. *'No goals were set, there was no checking to see whether we were complying with the ETI's requirements.'*[37] According to another, *'The most intensive social audit was done by the Co-op – their auditors came here for four days. But the others have mostly just been questionnaires.'* Furthermore, only 13 per cent of farm workers in South Africa recently surveyed had ever heard of codes of conduct, and just three per cent of them knew that codes related to workers' rights.[38] It is a lost opportunity for turning good codes into a tool to empower workers.

End the double standards!

Five purchasing practices which undermine labour standards in fresh-produce supply chains:

- placing same-day orders – common for airfreighted produce – that create erratic and unplanned overtime for women working in packhouses;

- demanding complex packaging and labelling requirements without reflecting the additional cost to producers in the price paid;

- using online auctions that put suppliers in tough competition on price, but without ensuring that ethical criteria are also met;

- breaking agreed orders at the last minute, forcing producers to turn to wholesale markets;

- using price-cutting promotions to hit the supermarkets' sales targets, but leaving farmers to bear the cost of lower prices.

Tesco, the UK's biggest and most profitable supermarket, promises customers that no one sells for less. But, as shown overleaf, Oxfam and partners' research in South Africa revealed that the purchasing practices used by Tesco – as well as by other supermarkets – are exacerbating the risks faced by farmers, leading to precarious jobs for the workers they employ.

Tesco

Kate Raworth

UK

Tesco is the UK's biggest and most profitable supermarket and is rapidly expanding overseas. But research by Oxfam and partners in South Africa reveals how Tesco loads many of the costs and risks of its fresh-produce business onto farmers, who are passing them on to workers – especially women – in the form of precarious employment.

Company information

Tesco had 26 per cent of the UK grocery market in 2003. The company sources products through suppliers in more than 100 countries and sells through 2,300 stores in 11 countries, including 83 hypermarkets in central Europe, 42 in Thailand, and 21 in South Korea. International sales in 2002–03 were US$ 49bn, and pre-tax profits were US$ 2.4bn.[39] Shareholders are reaping the rewards.

Keeping shareholders happy [40]

Chief Executive: Terry Leahy

The value of his employment contract in 2003 [41] includes:

● Base salary: £916,000 (US$1.6m)

● Performance-related bonuses: £1.85m (US$3.2m)

● Benefits including life assurance, disability and health insurance, and pension: £65,000 (US$111,000)

● Severance pay: two years' salary and double the annual bonus: £7.1m (US$12.2m)

Ethical trade policy

'Corporate Social Responsibility reflects our Values – treating people how we like to be treated.' [42]

'Our aim is to ensure that the working conditions of employees in companies that supply goods to Tesco meet or exceed relevant international labour standards. As founder Members of the Ethical Trading Initiative we have adopted the ETI's Base Code on labour standards as our benchmark. We are committed to sourcing only from primary sites that meet our standards and to ensure that those sites, in turn, promote these standards to their supply chain to achieve our ultimate goal.' [43]

To deliver these objectives, Tesco has an ethical trading programme which includes communicating its policy to suppliers; training technical managers, buyers, and suppliers in ethical sourcing issues; assessing and auditing supplying sites; and reviewing and reporting on progress internally and externally.[44] All suppliers must pay US$119 per quarter per site to pay for this programme. 'We wanted that to be at no extra cost to Tesco,' according to the head of the ethical trading programme.[45]

Pressures on South African fruit and wine producers

Basing producers' prices paid on target retail prices, not on production costs

'It's important that they [Tesco] actually realize what the true costs are. They start negotiating prices which are below production costs – that can't continue because you are going to force guys [farmers] out of business.' [46]
UK importer of South African fruit

Raising producers' costs without raising their prices

'Tesco wanted us to change their grape packaging from open to sealed bags. The new bags were three times as expensive – from 2.8 rand [US 44 cents] to 8 rand [US$ 1.2] per carton. And the productivity in the packhouse went through the floor, because it took workers 20 to 30 per cent longer to seal those bags. But the price stayed exactly the same – it wasn't even discussed. And then the other supermarkets all demanded it too. That's the way it goes.' [47]
table-grape farmer

Running promotions to capture market share – but making the farmer pay

'They also change the prices – £1.49 [US$ 2.55] is the price, then suddenly they put it on sale and make it 99p [US$1.70]. Then they sell it in bulk. The [technical] codes of conduct do not cost us half as much as these things do.' [48] apple farmer

Stripping out costs – and taking the savings

Tesco saved £200m (US$ 343m) in 2001/02 by cutting low-value-adding steps out of its supply chains. The company increasingly requires 'open book costing' – financial transparency – from suppliers. [49]

'They look at the cost chain and we have to declare all our costs and then they say "we don't need this cost" and it is cut. They heighten the risk but the sting in the tail is that they take 80 per cent or the entire amount of savings, with only a small proportion to the producers ... If you mention their margins, you run the risk of losing your toehold with them.' [50] packhouse manager

Charging fees to raise retail prices – e.g. from US$ 5.49 to US$5.99

'With the retailers it is really difficult. Just for them to take your wine from one level to another you have to give them £100,000 [US$170,000]. That bracket value can be as little as 50 pence [US 86 cents]. Tesco are like that – we basically have to subsidise our wine for them to sell it.' [51] wine producer

Focus on technical, not ethical, standards

Farmers are under pressure to meet the company's technical standards, but they report little pressure or reward for meeting ethical standards.

'Tesco never asked us about what we pay our labour or what our cottages [workers' housing] look like. That is up to our own conscience in terms of how we treat our labour.' [52] wine-grape grower

'We have met all the technical and social standards in Tesco's code but instead of buying more of our fruit, they still go to other farms around here that have not. And then they ask why we are supplying their competitors. What do they expect us to do?' [53] table-grape grower

Impacts on the farms' women workers

Growing use of temporary and contract labour

'There is less permanent labour, and fewer perks and lower increases for those that remain. This is a result of over-production and the suppression of prices by retailers,' said one apple farmer. Joanna, 40, has been a permanent worker on such a farm for 18 years and fears for the future. *'Many of the farmers are retrenching their permanent workers because they say they cannot afford it any more ... Where must we go?'*

Seasonal workers pay for social costs and risks

Women hired on seasonal contracts work 8 to 11 months of the year, year after year. *'They say we are "permanent contractors",'* said Analien, 42. Paid exactly the minimum wage, they cannot make ends meet, given the need to feed their children and pay schooling costs. As seasonal workers, most get no paid sick leave or maternity leave and no medical coverage. When children are sick, women must take unpaid time off. One visit to the doctor can cost 75 per cent of a week's earnings. Few are provided with protective clothing, fewer get any training.

'We have asked for protective clothing but ... they say it is too expensive for the farm and we should pay for the clothes.' Katryn, 35.

In season the women work 11 hours a day. Overtime is decided on the day, making childcare arrangements difficult. *'In the season there is a lot of pressure to meet the packhouse's deadlines, then we must work the whole day bent over in the sun,'* said Linkie, aged 50. *'We work in the rain ... and people get sick,'* said Joanna. *'We work in winter in the frost – but we must, because the day's totals must be made.'*

Appearances are maintained if Tesco's technologists visit.
'When Tesco say they are coming tomorrow then everything stops and we spend the whole day cleaning. ... Then we push all the portable toilets close to the road on the route that they will take. The toilets are never normally that clean.'
Saartjie, 30 [54]

South Africa

Paul Weinberg/OXFAM

Farm managers: passing it on to workers

Some farmers and growers have shown that respecting workers' rights and motivating them with training, equal opportunities, and secure jobs can increase quality and farm productivity – and they succeed in doing business this way. But commercial pressures from supermarkets and other industry buyers lead many to alternative strategies, especially when governments encourage it through weak implementation of the law. Under pressure on every issue but the way they treat their workers, far too many farmers and growers – in both rich and poor countries – hire women and migrants on insecure contracts, demand long hours on low pay, and intimidate workers out of speaking up.

Hiring women and migrants on insecure contracts

In flower and vegetable greenhouses – such as in Ecuador, Guatemala, Kenya, Mexico, and Zimbabwe – women are the majority of workers but are often hired repeatedly on short-term contracts. In sectors driven by seasons, such as fruit production, women are typically brought in for the seasonal jobs.[55] In Chile, women's employment in the fruit sector quadrupled between 1982 and 1992,[56] but they are heavily concentrated in temporary jobs and in 2001 one in two women workers had no written contract.[57]

Farm workers in Immokalee, Florida board buses at 4.30 am headed for a long day in the fields picking tomatoes

In rich countries, too, women and migrant workers fill the most precarious agricultural jobs. Fraser Valley, in Canada's province of British Columbia, is famous for its fruit farms but not for protecting its farmworkers, who are excluded from important labour laws in that province. Eighty per cent of the valley's fruit pickers are Punjabi, three-quarters of them women, mostly recent immigrants. Hired by contractors – usually Punjabi men – they work long hours on low piece-rates and are cheated out of overtime pay.[58] Likewise, Holland's flower industry – the biggest in the world – employs around 30,000 workers, two-thirds of them on temporary contracts, including significant numbers of illegal immigrants who have little power to claim their rights.[59]

Migrants now account for over half of all US farmworkers; three out of four of them are Mexican immigrants, often illegal, mostly young, single, and male. The law allows some in as temporary 'guest workers' but offers them little protection on arrival. Florida is one of the biggest users of agricultural labour and, like most other states, fails to cover farmworkers for the basic protections denied to them under federal law.[60] In the past six years there have been five federal prosecutions for slavery in Florida's agricultural sector against contractors who force illegal immigrants to work in the fields under threat of violence.[61]

Labour contractors, or gangmasters, are increasingly common. The cost savings to farmers of hiring through them were explained by one contractor in Chile:

'Outsourcing helps firms to optimise the use of human resources,' he said, 'given that it "eliminates deadweight" such as redundant payments due to work delays, or suspension of work due to weather conditions, and payments other than straight compensation.'[62] Some contractors operate legally and are registered; many are not. In parts of Chile, contractors are recruiting migrant women workers from Peru instead of local people. 'With the sub-contractors there isn't work,' said 35-year old Ximena, who has been picking grapes for three months a year since she was 17. 'They bring in people from outside, because they can cheat those people.'[63]

In South Africa's deciduous fruit sector, stronger labour legislation, combined with pressure from retailers, is leading farmers to cut back permanent jobs and hire temporary and contract labour instead. All deciduous fruit farmers and more than half of wine grape farmers interviewed in a 2001 study were using contractors for some of their hiring needs.[64] 'Bad market conditions resulted in layoffs, restructuring of the labour force and a move towards contract labour,' explained one apple farmer, who has halved his long-term workforce in the last five years and replaced them with contract workers. 'What has happened with labour is that you can cut them out at short notice if the business profitability decreases.'[65] The impacts on families can be severe. A study in 2003 found that more than one third of households in a fruit producing area reported the loss of a permanent job in the last five years, and one quarter of households were entirely dependent on earnings from seasonal or temporary labour.[66] The shift from on-farm to off-farm labour brings health risks: the HIV infection rate among on-farm households in 2002 was eight per cent, but workers are being moved off into settlements where the rate was 21 per cent.[67]

In the UK, a government investigation in 2003 revealed contractors illegally charging Chinese, Ukrainian, and Portuguese immigrants high recruitment fees to work excessive hours, picking fruit and flowers at piece-rates far below the minimum wage. It concluded that 'the dominant position of the supermarkets in relation to their suppliers is a significant contributory factor in creating an environment where illegal activity by gangmasters can take root. Intense price competition and the short time-scales between orders from the supermarkets ... put pressure on suppliers who have little opportunity or incentive to check the legality of labour which helps meet these orders.'[68]

With insecure jobs come insecure rights. Temporary, seasonal, and casual farm workers get fewer benefits and protections in most countries: entitled only to limited maternity leave and sick leave, often excluded from health and pension schemes, they have no access to benefits in-kind such as housing, transport, and food. 'Permanent workers are better off because they get to work until such time as they have to give birth and they come back to work,' said one migrant woman worker in South Africa, 'whereas temporary workers are sent straight back home and get replaced by someone else.'[69]

'Margins are so tight, we've got to survive and thus cut and restructure labour. You can't turn a packhouse on and off, you can't turn tractors on and off, you can't turn trees on and off, but you can turn people on and off.'

South African fruit-marketing agent

Temporary workers frequently cannot make enough payroll contributions to qualify for benefits. In Chile, the government addressed the problem in health-service access in 2002 by introducing a scheme for temporary workers, requiring only 60 days' worth of payroll contributions in return for year-round access to basic healthcare.[70] But the social security system still requires 20 years of full-time contributions to qualify for a pension. Temporary fruit workers, hired for just four months a year, cannot afford to contribute out of season. At 47, Rosa has been picking grapes during the harvest for 20 years, paying for food and the needs of her three children. *'It is impossible,'* she said. *'With so many children those gaps remain. I would need to have some money every month and I don't.'*[71] She would effectively have to work like this for 60 years to qualify.

Productivity, pressure, and pay

'Our company gets a higher price for flowers around Valentine's Day and Mother's Day. They should give us a bonus too, because their profits are thanks to our hard work.'[79]

Colombian flower worker

Farmworkers' wages cannot feed a family. In Colombia, women working in the flower sector are generally paid the minimum wage – but it covers only 45 per cent of a family's basic needs.[72] In 2003 the South African government introduced a minimum daily wage for agricultural workers for the first time, after campaigning by unions and NGOs – extending basic wage protection to some of the most vulnerable workers, including contract workers and migrants. But, according to campaigners, the minimum is still set according to what the industry will pay, not what workers need.[73] In the USA, piece-rates for tomato pickers have barely risen in 20 years; as a result of inflation, workers today are effectively paid 30 per cent less than they were in 1980.[74] There are gender gaps too: in Chile, women picking fruit commonly earn only three-quarters of men's wages for the same work. Now 55, Maria has been questioning this gap for almost 30 years of picking grapes, and she has asked for answers: *'There are many bosses who say "You can't earn more because you are a woman. What do you want more money for? It's the man who has to earn more",'* she said.[75]

Low piece-rates exert huge pressure on workers to earn enough. According to 46-year-old Ana, packing fruit in Chile, *'It depends on how fast you can work, you hurry as much as possible and run and try not to lose even a minute to earn more. We work against the clock – it's up to you how much salary you get. If you are slow, you'd better not work in a packing plant.'*[76] Some workers reported their employers fixing the books and adjusting piece-rates earned to meet only minimum wage levels. *'You're told you will earn so much per box,'* explained Ana, *'so you head off to work on that farm very satisfied, but once you are there, they don't pay you what you ought to get.'* [77] In Colombia, flower workers' production targets have been dramatically increased – from 24 flowerbeds in the 1980s to 42 beds today – but for the same pay.[78]

Long hours bring costs for many families. Luisa, a tomato picker in Florida, works on piece-rates for seven days a week, 11 hours a day at the height of the picking season: she should qualify for 148 hours of overtime pay a month, but US federal and state laws exclude farmworkers from that right. Workers like Luisa fear that their long hours away from home undermine their children's education. School enrolment rates for farmworkers' children are the lowest of all groups in the USA, with a high-school drop-out rate of 45 per cent.[80] Unsurprisingly, some of those children end up working alongside their parents: six per cent of the agricultural crop workers are 14–17 year-olds.[81]

Overtime is often far from voluntary: the requirements to meet shipping deadlines or same-day orders for just-in-time delivery frequently lead to compulsory late nights at short notice. Colombian flower workers can face up to six hours of overtime a day – despite a legal limit of two – especially in the peak seasons of Valentine's Day and Mother's Day. Now they will be paid less for it: the 2002 labour reform act shifted the start of overtime from 6pm to 10pm, effectively cutting women's pay for long days.[82] In fruit packhouses, complex packing and labelling requirements for different supermarkets slow down work. Combined with strict shipping deadlines, it can lead to up to eight hours of obligatory overtime a day, but paid at normal rates. *'We are often told on the same day that we have to work overtime that evening. It is then our responsibility to make arrangements with the [transport] services we use,'* explained one woman worker. *'We have to pay for the phone call ... Women who have children have to make special arrangements ... We are not given adequate warning to come to work prepared.'*[83]

Undermining unions, intimidating workers

Low rates of union membership undermine workers' attempts to call for better conditions. Some producers are determined to keep it that way. In Chile, workers fear being blacklisted by contractors if they speak out. Violeta, 47, is a member of a women farmworkers' union. *'If you make a claim,'* she said, *'you'll be fired by the contractor and he will pass the word to another contractor and will tell him "Listen, that old woman is a trouble maker". Then they'll tip each other off and you will not be hired.'*[84] Among Colombia's flower workers, 41 per cent of those interviewed believed they would be fired for joining a union, and 47 per cent did not want to discuss the issue.[85] Not surprising: Colombia is the most dangerous place in the world to be a trade union activist, with 189 death threats and 184 killings of trade unionists in 2002 alone.[86] Since 1993, the government of South Africa has been strengthening all agricultural workers' rights in law – but the reforms implicitly assume a 'big business, big union' industrial structure. Only six per cent of farmworkers are members of unions: many long-term workers are paid in-kind with on-farm housing and basic services, making independent organising difficult. And with few labour inspectors to ensure enforcement in this fragmented sector, farmworkers may still not get adequate protection in practice.[87]

'Once, we started at ten in the morning and finished at six in the morning the next day ... since it is so far away and since there is no transportation, you cannot say, "This is it, I'm going home".'[88]

Maria, 47, sub-contracted to pick grapes for Dole in Chile

'As women and as workers, we have to fight for our rights and against violence both in the fields and in our homes.'

Julia Gabriel of the Coalition of Immokalee Workers, Florida tomato pickers

5

Making trade work
for women as workers

Kenyan women and men walk to the garment factories because monthly bus fares would cost around 25 per cent of their wages. A network of local NGOs and unions is supporting workers like these by campaigning for their rights to living wages, paid maternity leave, and the freedom to join trade unions without intimidation.

5 Making trade work for women as workers

Trade can work for women workers, their families, and communities. A job in a garment factory or on a fruit farm could be the job that provides a woman with the income, security, and support that she needs to become empowered in her household and community and to ensure a better future for her children. What is needed to make it happen? Three priorities:

Empowering workers to defend their rights and interests

Workers' rights will never be realised unless workers are empowered to defend them. They are the only people who know the day-to-day realities of their jobs. They are the best people to negotiate what would be a fair wage and a decent limit on overtime in their industry and country. And their involvement is central to making both legal and voluntary mechanisms to enable workers' rights to function effectively. That is why respect for the right to association, to join trade unions, and to bargain collectively is central.

Ensuring voluntary initiatives strengthen respect for international labour standards

Many international human rights and labour conventions are obligatory for all countries – and the best means of complying with them is legislative protection. Voluntary mechanisms must strengthen, rather than substitute for these. Retailers' and brand companies' initiatives – such as codes of conduct – can be helpful tools only if they are based on international labour standards, if they involve and empower workers in claiming their rights, and if they lead companies to address the impact of their own purchasing practices on labour standards in the supply chain.

Sharing the costs of caring work

Women have too long been made to pay for the social costs of 'flexible' labour markets at the expense of their own health, gender equality, and their families' future prospects. Missing from official statistics, these costs are effectively a hidden subsidy to the retailers and brands in whose supply chains women work. For governments, flexibility may bring a short-term competitive advantage, but it could also create a long-term liability for human development and gender equality. Policies and practices are urgently needed which promote a more equitable distribution of the costs of caring work among women and men, employers and the State.

Recommendations

No single company or government can make the changes needed to ensure that poor people, and especially women, benefit from jobs in global supply chains. But together the initiatives of companies, governments, international institutions, consumers, and investors can make all the difference. Oxfam and partners call on them to take urgent action so that women's precarious jobs turn into empowering jobs.

Companies in the supply chain: retail and brand sourcing companies

Until companies recognise that their own sourcing and purchasing practices are one of the root causes of poor labour standards, they will not resolve the problems in their supply chains. The best codes of conduct explicitly recognise the need for sourcing companies to address their own purchasing practices in order to ensure that labour standards are respected. The Fair Wear Foundation specifies that 'The buying/outsourcing policy of the member company must explicitly take into account that the terms of trade offered to suppliers will not impede the supplier's implementation of the Fair Wear Labour Standards.'[3] Likewise the Ethical Trading Initiative requires that 'The code and the implementation process is integrated into the core business relationships and culture ... Negotiations with suppliers shall take into account the costs of observing the code.'[4] Some companies have started tackling the problem, showing that it is possible to make a difference. It is up to each company to find ways to:

- promote workers' empowerment throughout the supply chain
- make respect for workers' rights integral to the company's vision
- integrate that commitment into purchasing practices.

Promote workers' empowerment throughout the supply chain

- Adopt a clear commitment, at the highest level of corporate management, to respect international labour standards throughout the supply chain.

- Conduct workplace inspections in conjunction with workers, trade unions, and credible local organisations. Ensure that inspections address any restrictions on trade unions; access to paid maternity leave, sick leave, and annual leave; employment terms for workers on temporary contracts, home workers, and sub-contracting; overtime payments, piece-rates, and performance targets.

- Engage in constructive dialogue with global union federations and establish ongoing dialogue about the rights of workers in the company's supply chains worldwide.

Make respect for workers' rights integral to the company's vision

- Ensure in-house expertise on ethical issues, and make those staff equal in corporate hierarchy to buyers. Addressing purchasing practices should be a central part of their mandate.
- Ensure that buyers' and managers' incentives and performance assessments are structured to reward, rather than undermine, ethical purchasing. And train buyers to be aware of the possible impacts of their negotiations on labour standards.
- Make a commitment to adopt a mechanism to communicate the place and method of production, and to being transparent about business operations to consumers and shareholders.

Integrate that commitment into purchasing practices in the four following areas:
1 Making labour standards a key sourcing criterion

- Make 'good or improving labour standards' a criterion equal in importance to quality and delivery in selecting and assessing producers.
- Give approved producers – with good or improving labour standards – the status of being preferred suppliers.
- Work towards buying only from approved producers, and support them in the approval process.

2 Setting adequate delivery lead times

- Ensure that internal procedures for placing orders do not create excessive or unagreed time pressures for producers.
- Share order-scheduling information with producers to enable them to plan better.
- Repay the costs incurred by producers due to significant delays and changes made by the company in the process of placing orders.

3 Negotiating fair prices

- Ensure that pricing is compatible with the producer meeting international labour standards, including:
  - where the risk of price fluctuations is carried by the producer, pay a price that reflects that additional risk;
  - ensure that price negotiation methods do not undermine the feasibility of the producer complying with those standards.

4 Working with producers

- Build stable long-term relationships with producers, so they have the incentive to invest in improving labour standards – and if meeting those standards requires higher prices, continue to source from that producer.

- Support producers where necessary in building their managerial capacity, and ensure that workers benefit from any productivity improvements.

- Give producers opportunities to provide feedback on the pressures that they face without jeopardising their contractual relationship.

Companies in the supply chain: producers and suppliers

Better farm and factory management is often the most immediate step towards better employment and working conditions. Owners and managers must:

- Commit themselves to providing terms of employment and working conditions that comply with international labour standards and national laws, whichever provides workers with higher protection.

- Ensure especially that women workers' interests are protected by:

  - promoting equal opportunities in the workplace and ensuring that workers have access to childcare facilities, lighter duties for women during pregnancy, and breast-feeding breaks for mothers;

  - transferring workers repeatedly hired on short-term contracts onto long-term contracts so that they receive their rightful benefits;

  - extending employment benefits to all categories of workers, especially paid maternity leave, annual leave, and sick leave, in proportion to their time worked.

Good initiatives in sourcing and purchasing practices

Some companies have recognised and started to tackle some of the problems created by their purchasing practices. On a wider scale, the following initiatives could help to bring significant improvements in employment and working conditions:

Reviewing ordering processes: the Swedish fashion retailer, H&M, is reviewing its own ordering practices after several months of excessive overtime in two suppliers' factories in China and Turkey. '*There are so many people involved here at H&M – technicians, quality control, merchandisers, and compliance – that no one in our company has the full picture of how the orders went from beginning to end,*' said Ingrid Schullstrom, Manager of Corporate Social Responsibility. '*So we are reviewing what happened during those months – were there late approvals or fabric delays or quality problems? Were we part of the problem here? We need to understand the full picture and then work internally and with our suppliers towards a sustainable solution.*' [5] Marks and Spencer, a major UK retailer, is far into this process of 'critical path management' for its garment supply chains. '*One major reason for long hours in factories is poor production planning – and responsibility for that starts back with us,*' said Muriel Johnson, Head of Social Compliance. In early 2003 the company enhanced its online database for tracking the status of worldwide orders, by including key dates and responsibilities for making internal decisions, to ensure that producers' lead times are not cut short. [6]

Priority to approved producers: Premier Brands sells tea to several UK supermarkets, sourced from more than 150 estates in 12 countries.

By building long-term relationships with producers and paying for the social audits, the company is moving towards buying only from approved producers. '*Five years ago, around 60 per cent of our suppliers were approved – today it is almost 90 per cent,*' said Michael Pennant-Jones, Ethical Sourcing Manager. '*And getting on our approved supplier list acts as a carrot for producers to raise their labour standards.*'

Working with global unions: in 2001, the banana company, Chiquita, signed an international framework agreement with the International Union Federation (IUF) for food and agriculture. The agreement creates a forum for addressing workers' rights violations arising in the company's worldwide operations and supply chains. '*Multinational companies make strategic decisions at the global level, but most refuse to accept global responsibility for industrial relations,*' said Peter Rossman, Communications Director at the IUF. '*That is why agreements like this one are a valuable tool for bringing industrial relations into the new environment of globalised production.*' [7]

Supply chain transparency: in 2002, more than 20 major clothing retailers in Australia, including the Cole Myers Group (with Target and Kmart) and David Jones, signed up to a code for ethical retailers, and now provide the Australian clothing and footwear union, TCFUA, with details of their in-country suppliers, prices paid, and turn-around times demanded. Linking this to information from suppliers and producers who have likewise signed up to codes, the union now has detailed and current data on these supply chains. Although the agreement covers only clothing made in Australia, it is an important precedent for greater transparency on purchasing practices. [8]

National governments

Protect the rights of workers by ensuring that labour legislation consistent with international labour standards is enacted, implemented, and enforced. In order, especially, to ensure that women's jobs in global supply chains are empowering, not precarious:

- Ensure that all workers can, in practice, join trade unions and bargain collectively without fear or reprisal.
- Extend labour-law protections and benefits to cover all categories of workers so that, for example, temporary and homeworking contracts are not misused to avoid paying benefits.
- Strengthen laws and policies concerning sexual harassment, health and safety at work, and maternity and childcare provision to reflect women workers' specific needs.
- Strengthen labour inspectorates and worker complaint mechanisms so that they are more responsive to the challenges facing women workers.
- Ensure that domestically registered companies, including mid-chain suppliers, conduct their international business operations in ways that respect workers' rights in law.

The ILO and the WTO

- Member governments should increase their funding and support to the ILO, in order to strengthen its supervisory and capacity-building role in supporting national efforts to comply with ILO conventions.
- The WTO must acknowledge that trade rules do not have primacy over international human rights and labour conventions, and that legitimate ILO-endorsed trade sanctions – such as in the case of Burma – cannot be challenged as an unacceptable barrier to trade under WTO rules.
- Coordination between the ILO and WTO should be formally strengthened to address the relationship between trade rules and workers' rights and livelihoods.
- The WTO's Trade Policy Reviews should include reports, produced by the ILO, on the impact of trade rules and practices on employment standards, and in particular on women workers. In the mean time, Oxfam welcomes the initiative of the ICFTU in submitting reports on these issues.

The World Bank, IMF, and Regional Development Banks

- Actively support and promote respect for internationally agreed core labour standards as a means to poverty reduction, not only at headquarters but also in country-level operations, and through all lending programmes.

- Take full account of the gender, social, and economic impacts of advice and conditions given regarding labour reforms, and consult with the ILO to ensure that loan conditions do not undermine labour rights or gender equity.

- Support strengthening the capacity of government ministries and agencies that are responsible for ensuring those laws are enforced.

- Call on international and local business communities to take responsibility for the impacts on workers of the way that they do business through their supply chains.

Institutional investors

The socially responsible investment (SRI) movement is growing rapidly, and is screening or engaging with publicly listed companies on ethical concerns, including labour standards in the supply chain. SRI in the USA has more than doubled since 1995, with total funds exceeding US$2 trillion by 2003.[9] In Canada, SRI funds passed US$50bn in 2002[10], and in 2003 Europe's SRI market was worth US$390bn.[11] In Australia and Japan too, SRI funds were worth US$14bn and US$1bn respectively.[12] Labour standards were one of the first issues tackled and are still high on the agenda. But most SRI firms still benchmark companies only in terms of having a good code of conduct and making efforts to monitor producers' compliance with it. They can now play a leading role in taking the labour standards agenda forward by:

- strengthening the benchmarking criteria used to include evidence of credible and identifiable steps by retailers and brands to address any harmful impacts of their purchasing practices;

- engaging with those companies on the initiatives that they are taking and the outcomes achieved for workers in their supply chains.

Consumers

The ethical consumer movement began with fair trade: in the late 1990s, worldwide fair-trade sales reached US$400m for around 100 products.[13] Now the movement has gone a step further, pushing for ethical standards in all supply chains. For retailers and brands, the consumer is king – and consumers can use that status to:

- Buy fair trade products, to send a loud signal to retailers that consumers care and are willing to pay for decent labour standards.
- Demand that retailer and brand companies adopt a clear commitment to implement international labour standards in all their supply chains, as outlined in model codes, and ensure adequate monitoring and independent verification.
- Demand that companies ensure that their purchasing practices do not undermine those commitments.
- Demand that companies are transparent about where and how their products are made, about their policies and practices, and about the impacts of these upon employment terms and working conditions in their supply chains.

Appendix

Oxfam and partners

Oxfam works with more than 60 partner organisations across the world to address issues of labour rights. Research for this report was conducted in 12 countries, in which the following organisations are among Oxfam's partners:

Bangladesh

The Make Trade Fair Alliance consists of 12 organisations working together to fight unfair global trade rules and their consequences in Bangladesh. The Alliance focuses on protecting the livelihoods of garment workers, and among them INCIDIN Bangladesh, Karmojibi Nari, and Garments Sramic Okkya Parishad are directly involved with women workers.

Chile

Oxfam's partners addressing women workers' rights include Hexagrama, engaged in research and policy; CEM, conducting research and advocacy; ANAMURI, organising and representing rural and indigenous women; La Morada, focused on social, economic, and cultural rights; CEDEM, researching the agro-export sector; and Mujer y Trabajo, raising awareness of social security issues for seasonal workers.

China

Research in Hong Kong and in Guangdong, China, was conducted by the Institute of Contemporary Observation, Chinese Working Women's Network, Hong Kong Women Workers' Association, and the Clothing, Clerical and Retail Employees' General Union, CCRGU. All four organisations provide legal services, conduct training in workers' rights and public education, and do research on issues related to women workers, including garment workers.

Colombia

Corporación Cactus is an NGO focused on social, environmental, and work-related impacts of the cut-flower export industry. Its activities include research, legal consultancy, and awareness raising campaigns supporting flower workers and other residents of flower-producing municipalities.

Honduras

The Coalition for Labour Rights in Honduras brings together organisations seeking alternative ways to promote the rights of women working in the garment sector. They include CODEMUH, CDM, and ERIC supporting, organising, and educating women workers; CJP, which provides legal advice; and workers' trade unions such as CGT and CUTH.

Kenya

The Kenya Human Rights Commission is a non-government membership organisation founded in 1992 with a mission to promote, protect, and enhance the enjoyment of all human rights in Kenya. KHRC does this through education and outreach, monitoring and documenting violations, and advocacy work.

Morocco

CDG is a human rights organisation managing a centre for supporting women workers in Fes. La Chabaka is a network of more than 55 NGOs in the north of Morocco, supporting women workers in Tangier. The AMDF and the LDDF are two women's rights organisations interested in labour rights for women as part of their fight for a human rights conception of women's rights.

Sri Lanka

The Sri Lanka Labour Rights Core Group currently consists of three trade unions: Free Trade Zone Workers' Union, Progress Union, and Eksath Kamkaru Sangamaya; five labour NGOs: Kalape Api, Women's Center, Dabindu Collective, Young Christian Workers, and Shramabini Kendraya; with the Fredrich Ebert Stiftung and the American Solidarity Center as observers. Together they are running a campaign on the burning issues faced by women workers in the garment industry threatened by the phasing out of the Multi-Fibre Arrangement.

South Africa

Women on Farms Project (WFP) organises women workers and their families in the wine and deciduous fruit sectors of the Western Cape, building organisation and developing the capacity of women to campaign for better working and living conditions, especially for women seasonal agricultural workers.

Thailand

The Thai Labour Working Group brings together labour organisations committed to promoting workers' rights. It includes the Thai Labour Campaign, HomeNet Thailand, Lawyers Council of Thailand, The Center for Labour Information Service and Training, Women Workers in Unity Group, Thai Labour Solidarity Committee, Arom Pongpangan Foundation, Textile, Garment, and Leather Workers' Federation of Thailand, Labour Coordinating Centre, American Centre for International Labour Solidarity (ACILS), and the Committee for Asian Women.

UK

The National Group on Homeworking is the only national NGO working solely for the benefit of UK homeworkers. NGH is a membership organisation that counts homeworkers, local homeworking projects, trade unions, local authorities, and policy makers among its membership.

USA

The Farm Labor Organizing Committee (FLOC) seeks to improve working conditions for migrant farmworkers. FLOC is pressuring Mt. Olive Pickle to increase the price it pays to workers in the USA, Sri Lanka, and India. The Coalition of Immokalee Workers seeks to improve labour conditions for farmworkers in Florida. CIW is pressuring Taco Bell to pay workers a penny more per pound of tomatoes picked.

Background research reports

Barkat, A., S. N. Ahmed, A.K.M. Maksud, and M. A. Ali (2003) 'The Cost for Women Workers of Precarious Employment in Bangladesh', Human Development Research Centre, Dhaka: Oxfam GB.

Belghazi, S. (2003) 'The Sportswear Value Chain in Morocco', Madrid: Oxfam Intermón.

CEDEM (2003) 'Consequences and Costs of Precarious Employment for Women Workers in the Chilean Agro-exports Sector', Santiago: Oxfam GB and Oxfam Canada.

Centre for Policy Alternatives (2003) 'Women Workers and the Garment Industry in Sri Lanka', Colombo: Oxfam Community Aid Abroad.

Colectivo Al Jaima and La Chabaka (2003) 'The Global Production Network of El Corte Inglés in Morocco', research coordinator E. Maleno, Madrid: Oxfam Intermón.

Cunliffe, L. (2003) 'The Garment Sector Business Model for Purchasing Practices Throughout the Supply Chain', Oxford: Oxfam GB.

Diaz, E. (2003) 'Fruit Exporters' Purchasing Practices in Chile', Santiago: Oxfam GB and Oxfam Canada.

Goldstein, B. and J.B. Leonard (2003) 'Injustices in the Fields, Injustice in the Law: Farmworkers in the United States', Boston: Oxfam America.

Herrera, B., with L. Puyo, O. Londoño, J. Vidal Castaño, and N. Soto (2003) 'Study of Women Workers' Rights in the Colombian Flower Industry', Bogotá: Oxfam GB.

Kamungi, P. and S. Ouma (2003) 'The Manufacture of Poverty: the Untold Story of EPZs in Kenya', Kenya Human Rights Commission, Nairobi: NOVIB.

Kruger, S. (2003)'Interviews with Seasonal Women Farm Workers in South Africa', Stellenbosch: NOVIB.

Lee, R. and P. Wannaboriboon (2003) 'Global Trade and Women Workers in Thailand', Homenet Thailand, Bangkok: Oxfam GB.

Liu, K.M. (2003) 'Research Report on Global Purchasing Practices and Chinese Women Workers', Institute of Contemporary Observation, Hong Kong: Oxfam Hong Kong.

López, D. (2003) 'Overview of Chilean Labour Law', Santiago: Oxfam GB and Oxfam Canada.

Martinez, M.A. (2003) 'Labour Laws in Honduras', Tegulcigalpa: Oxfam GB.

Mather, C. and S. Greenberg (2003) Unpublished interview transcripts with South African farmers.

Mattera, P. and M. Khan (2003) 'Report on Supply Chain Dynamics for Fresh Tomatoes and Pickling Cucumbers in the United States', Boston: Oxfam America.

Meesit, C. (2003) 'Legal Principles of the Labour Laws in Thailand', Bangkok: Oxfam GB.

Mejjati Alami, R. (2003) 'Fair Trade, Gender and Labour Rights in Morocco', Madrid: Oxfam Intermón.

Moher, G. (2003) 'Farmworkers in the Fraser Valley of British Colombia', Ottawa: Oxfam Canada.

National Group on Homeworking (2003) 'Homeworkers in the UK', Oxford: Oxfam GB.

Ortez, O. (2003) 'Purchasing Practices in Global Value Chains that Result in Precarious Employment: the Case of Honduran Maquilas', Tegulcigalpa: Oxfam GB.

Pérez, T.B., V. Hernández, K. Lorena Altamirano, and O. Altamirano (2003) 'Women in the Maquila – At What Price?', Tegucigalpa: Oxfam GB.

Pun, N. (2003) 'The Precarious Employment and Hidden Costs of Women Workers in Shenzhen', The Chinese Working Women Network, Hong Kong: Oxfam Hong Kong.

Rahman, M., M.R. Ullah, and A. Ali (2003) 'Labour Law Research for Bangladesh', Human Development Research Centre, Dhaka: Oxfam GB.

Sayer, G. (2003) 'Interviews with Garment Workers in Kenya's Export Processing Zones', Oxford: Oxfam GB.

Women on Farms (2003) 'Women Workers in Wine and Deciduous Fruit Global Value Chains', Stellenbosch: NOVIB.

Yimprasert, L. and Thai Labour Campaign (2003) 'Supply Chain in the Thai Garment Industry: the Impact on Workers!', Bangkok: Oxfam GB.

Acronyms

AGOA	Africa Growth and Opportunity Act
COFESA	Confederation of Employers of South Africa
EPZ	export processing zone
ETI	Ethical Trading Initiative
EU	European Union
FAO	Food and Agriculture Organization
ICFTU	International Confederation of Free Trade Unions
ILO	International Labour Organization
IMF	International Monetary Fund
IUF	International Union of Food, Agricultural, Hotel, Restaurant, Catering, Tobacco and Allied Workers' Associations
MFA	Multi-Fibre Arrangement, or Multi-Fibre Agreement
NAFTA	North American Free Trade Agreement
NGO	non-government organisation
TCFUA	Textile, Clothing, and Footwear Union of Australia
TNC	transnational company
WTO	World Trade Organization

Notes

1 Women on Farms (2003)

2 Oxfam interview 3 July 2003

3 Collectivo Al Jaima and La Chabaka (2003)

4 P. Krugman (1997) 'In praise of cheap labour', *Slate* 20 March

5 D. Birnbaum (2001) 'The coming garment massacre', *Canadian Apparel Magazine* November–December 2001 www.apparel.ca/magazine/2001Dec/Garment%20Massacre.pdf

Chapter 1

1 G. Sayer (2003)

2 B. Herrera et al. (2003)

3 J. Ramsey (2003) 'Improving Labour Rights for Women Maquila Workers', Oxford: Oxfam GB

4 Zohir and Paul-Majumder (1996) 'Garment Workers in Bangladesh: Economic, Social and Health Conditions', Research monograph no. 18, Dhaka: Bangladesh Institute of Development Studies

5 N. Kabeer (2000) *The Power to Choose*, London: Verso

6 A. Barkat et al. (2003)

7 Oxfam interview 17 November 2003

8 Based on D. Elson (1999) 'Labour markets at gendered institutions: equality, efficiency and empowerment issues', *World Development* 27(3), and M. Williams (2003) *Gender Mainstreaming in the Multilateral Trading System*, The Commonwealth Secretariat: London

9 ILO (2003) *Working Out of Poverty*, Geneva: ILO

10 Women on Farms (2003)

11 National Group on Homeworking (2003), and Oxfam interview 17 November 2003

12 A. Barkat et al. (2003)

13 CEDEM (2003)

14 P. Kamungi and S. Ouma (2003)

15 Cisadane Labour Committee (2003) 'Initial Findings of Investigation by the Cisadane Labour Committee into the Contract Work System', unpublished report, Indonesia

16 C. Skinner and I. Valodia (2002) 'Labour Market Policy, Flexibility, and the Future of Labour Relations: the Case of KwaZulu-Natal Clothing Industry', *Transformation* (50)

17 B. Herrera et al. (2003) and Oxfam interview 24 November 2003

18 Oxfam interview 24 November 2003

19 B. Herrera et al. (2003)

20 Women on Farms (2003)

21 K.A. Ver Beek (2001) 'Maquiladoras: exploitation or emancipation? An overview of the situation of maquiladora workers in Honduras', *World Development* 29(9)

22 A. Barkat et al. (2003)

23 D. López (2003)

24 National Group on Homeworking (2003)

25 Oxfam interview 10 November 2003

26 Liu, K.M. (2003)

27 Pun, N. (2003)

28 Centre for Policy Alternatives (2003)

29 Colectivo Al Jaima and La Chabaka (2003)

30 Calculation by Oxfam based on research interviews

31 A. Barkat et al. (2003)

32 Oxfam interview 2 July 2003

33 T.B. Pérez et al. (2003)

34 S. Smith, D. Auret, S. Barrientos, C. Dolan, K. Kleinbooi, C. Njobvu, M. Opondo, and A. Tallontire (2003) 'Ethical Trade in African Horticulture: Gender, Rights and Participation', Institute of Development Studies, Sussex. Preliminary report for multi-stakeholder workshop, 26 June 2003

35 Women on Farms (2003)

36 P. Kamungi and S. Ouma (2003)

37 International Confederation of Free Trade Unions (2003) 'Discussion Guide', 8th World Women's Conference, Melbourne, Australia, 18–21 February 2003

38 ILO 'Promoting Gender Equality', Booklet 6: 'Alliances and Solidarity to Promote Women Workers' Rights', ILO: Geneva

39   Womyn's Agenda for Change (2002) 'A Social Study of Women Workers in the Cambodian Garment Industry', www.womynsagenda.org

40   N. Pandey (2003) 'Case Study on Female Garment Workers in Bangalore', Hyderabad: Oxfam GB

41   P. Kamungi and S. Ouma (2003)

42   Womyn's Agenda for Change (2002) op.cit.

43   Oxfam interview 9 December 2002

44   G. Moher (2003)

45   V. Meier (1999) 'Cut-flower production in Colombia: a major development success story for women?' *Environment and Planning* 31: 273–89

46   Colectivo Al Jaima and La Chabaka (2003)

47   National Group on Homeworking (2003)

48   P.K. Mills and S. Kwong (2001) 'Cancer incidence in the United Farm Workers of America (UFW) 1987–1997', *American Journal of Industrial Medicine* 40:596–603

49   Green (1995) cited in S. Barrientos, A. Bee, A. Matear, and I. Vogel (1999) *Women and Agribusiness: Working Miracles in the Chilean Fruit Export Sector*, Basingstoke: Macmillan

50   Riquelme (2000) cited in CEDEM (2003)

51   Centre for Policy Alternatives (2003)

52   Solomon (2000) cited in Goldstein and Leonard (2003)

53   Colectivo Al Jaima and La Chabaka (2003)

54   B. Herrera et al. 2003

55   A. Barkat et al. 2003

56   D. Elson (1999) op. cit.

57   Womyn's Agenda for Change (2001) op. cit.

58   N. Folbre (1994) *Who Pays for the Kids? Gender and the Structures of Constraint*, London: Routledge

59   A. Barkat et al. (2003)

60   V. Meier (1999) op. cit.

61   A. Barkat et al. (2003)

62   Womyn's Agenda for Change (2002) op. cit.

63   Centre for Policy Alternatives (2003)

64   P. Kamungi and S. Ouma (2003)

Chapter 2

1   Oxfam interview 23 October 2003

2   World Bank (2003) *Global Economic Prospects and the Developing Countries*, Washington D.C.: World Bank

3   Ibid.

4   G. Gereffi (1999), 'International Trade and Industrial Upgrading in the Apparel Commodity Chain', *Journal of International Economics* 48: 37–70

5   Wal-Mart Investor information. www.walmart.com 10 November 2003

6   P. Wonacott (2003) 'Wilting plants – behind China's export boom, heated battle among factories', *Wall Street Journal* 13 November 2003

7   S. Greenhouse (2003) 'Wal-Mart, driving workers and supermarkets crazy', *New York Times* 19 October 2003

8   M. Garrahan (2003) 'How to keep doing it all over the world', *Financial Times* 5 August 2003

9   SOMO (2003) *Bulletin on Issues in Garments and Textiles* No. 2 July 2003

10   J. Magretta (1998) 'Fast, global and entrepreneurial: supply chain management Hong Kong style. An interview with Victor Fung', *Harvard Business Review* http://harvardbusinessonline.hbsp.harvard.edu/

11   World Bank (2003) op. cit.

12   H. Schmitz and P. Knorringa (2000) 'Learning from global buyers', *Journal of Development Studies* 37 (2)

13   The analytical framework is derived from P. Gibbon and S. Ponte (forthcoming) *Trading Down: Africa, Value Chains and the Global Economy*

14   E. Millstone and T. Lang (2003) *The Atlas of Food*, London: Earthscan

15   Oxfam interview 23 October 2003

16   Oxfam interview 7 November 2003

17   Pun, N. (2003)

18   ILO (1998) 'Declaration on Fundamental Principles and Rights at Work',

www.ilo.org/public/english/standards/decl/
declaration/text/tindex.htm

19 These are the standards that comprise the Base
    Code of the UK's Ethical Trading Initiative

20 The American Chamber of Commerce-PRC (2002)
    'White Paper: American Business in China'
    www.amchamchina.org.cn/publications/white/2002/
    en-9.htm

21 Colectivo Al Jaima and La Chabaka (2003)

22 Comment made by James Wolfensohn in dialogue
    with ICFTU. Reported in
    www.multinationalmonitor.org/mm2001/01septemb
    er/sep01corp1.html

23 A. Toke and Z. Tzannatos (2003) Unions and
    Collective Bargaining: Economic Effects in a Global
    Environment, Washington D.C.: World Bank

24 ICFTU Press Release 'World Bank Highlights Positive
    Development Impact of Trade Unions', 12 February
    2003

25 ICFTU Press Release 'Trade Unions Welcome
    Breakthrough on Workers' Rights at World Bank', 23
    September 2003

26 World Bank (2002) 'Country Assistance Strategy –
    Mexico 2002'

27 IMF (2002) 'Article IV Consultation, Chile', 2002
    www.imf.org/external/pubs/cat/longres.cfm?sk=152
    43.0

28 IMF (2002) 'Colombia – Letter of Intent,
    Memorandum of Economic Policy and Technical
    Memorandum of Understanding 2002',
    www.imf.org/external/np/loi/2002/col/01/index.htm

29 World Bank (1996) 'Bangladesh – Labour Market
    Policies for Higher Employment', World Bank Sector
    Report, Washington DC: World Bank

30 ILO (2002) 'Employment and Social Policy in
    Respect of Export Processing Zones' GB.285/ESP/5.
    Geneva November 2002

31 A. Beattie (2003) 'Report casts doubt on FDI
    incentives', Financial Times 15 October 2003

32 World Bank (2003) op. cit.

33 World Bank (2003) op. cit.

34 Shenzhen Labour Bureau (1992) 'Shenzhen Tequ
    Laodong Zhidu Shinian Gaige Licheng (Ten Years of
    Reform of the Labour System in the Shenzhen
    EPZ)', Shenzhen: Haitian Press, cited in Pun, (2003)

35 ICFTU (2003) Annual Survey of Violations of Trade
    Union Rights, Brussels: ICFTU

36 ICFTU (2003) op. cit.

Chapter 3

1   P. Gibbon (2003) 'At the Cutting Edge? UK Clothing
    Retailers' Global Sourcing Patterns and Practices
    and Their Implications for Developing Countries',
    Copenhagen: Centre for Development Research

2   SOMO (2003) Bulletin on Issues in Garments and
    Textiles, no. 2 July 2003

3   Euromonitor, cited in C. Pope Murray (2001)
    Salomon Smith Barney Equity Research, 'Crossing
    the Pond: European Growth Strategies', 23 October
    2001

4   The 100 top brands', Business Week 4 August 2003,
    www.businessweek.com/pdfs/2003/0331_globalbra
    nds.pdf

5   UNCTAD (2002) 'World Investment Report:
    Transnational Corporations and Export
    Competitiveness', UNCTAD: Geneva

6   Euromonitor (2001) Retail Trade International 2001

7   SOMO (2003) Bulletin on Issues in Garments and
    Textiles No. 2, July 2003

8   www.just-style.com (2003) 'European Apparel
    Retailers Face Rocky Road', 25 March 2003

9   Mintel International (2000) 'Department and Variety
    Store Retailing – Spain; Portugal'
    http://www.marketresearch.com/researchindex/727
    525.html

10 Bureau van Djik (2003), 'Company Report for El
    Corte Inglés S.A.', AMADEUS database,
    http://www.bvdep.com

11 Colectivo Al Jaima and La Chabaka (2003)

12 Research by Sam Grumiau for ICFTU, October 2003

13 E. Mariani (2003) 'Korean investors reluctant to
    enter RI', Jakarta Post 3 June 2003

14 Pun, N. (2003)

15 Cotton Incorporated (2003) 'Spinning responds: the upstream effects of retail deflation and imports' *Textile Consumer* Vol. 29, Spring 2003

16 Ibid.

17 Oxfam interview 18 October 2003

18 Oxfam interviews October 2003

19 Liu, K.M. (2003)

20 Wal-Mart Investor Information, 10 November 2003, www.walmart.com.

21 G. Sayer (2003)

22 P. Kamungi and S. Ouma (2003)

23 Wick (2003) *Worker's Tool or PR Ploy? A Guide to Codes of International Labour Practice*, Germany: Friedrich Ebert Stiftung

24 www.eti.org.uk

25 www.fairwear.nl

26 www.workersrights.org

27 www.fairlabor.org

28 www.cepaa.org

29 O. Ortez (2003)

30 Centre for Policy Alternatives (2003)

31 Oxfam interview 3 July 2003

32 Oxfam interview 3 July 2003

33 Centre for Policy Alternatives (2003)

34 D. Drickhamer (2002) 'Under fire', *Industry Week* 1 June 2002 www.iwvaluechain.com/Features/articles.asp?Article ld=1262

35 Centre for Policy Alternatives (2003), and A. Barkat et al. (2003)

36 Womyn's Agenda for Change (2002) op.cit.

37 Liu, K.M. (2003)

38 T.B. Pérez et al. (2003)

39 Centre for Policy Alternatives (2003)

40 Oxfam interview 2 July 2003

41 Colectivo Al Jaima and La Chabaka (2003)

42 Centre for Policy Alternatives (2003)

43 Colectivo Al Jaima and La Chabaka (2003)

44 Centre for Policy Alternatives (2003)

45 O.Ortez (2003)

46 Centre for Policy Alternatives (2003)

47 Centre for Policy Alternatives (2003)

48 S. Belghazi (2003)

49 P. Kamungi and S. Ouma (2003)

50 Centre for Policy Alternatives (2003)

51 ICFTU (2003) 'Philippines: a union awakening in the export processing zones', August 2003 No. 5

52 R. Lee and P. Wannaboriboon (2003)

53 T.B. Pérez et al. (2003)

54 Centre for Policy Alternatives (2003)

55 Pun, N. (2003)

56 C. Meesit (2003)

57 A. Rahman et al. (2003)

58 N. Pandey (2003) 'Case Study on Female Garment Workers in Bangalore' Hyderabad: Oxfam GB

Chapter 4

1   C. Dolan and K. Sorby (2003) 'Gender and Employment in High-value Agricultural and Rural Industries', Agriculture and Rural Development Working Paper Series No. 7, Washington, DC: World Bank

2   B. Herrera et al. (2003)

3   C. Dolan and K. Sorby (2003) op.cit.

4   Women on Farms (2003), and correspondence with the Deciduous Fruit Producers Trust

5   B. Goldstein and J.B. Leonard (2003)

6   F. Brassel and C.E. Rangel (2001) 'Flowers for Justice: Implementing the International Code of Conduct', FIAN, Germany

7   Women on Farms (2003)

8   P. Mattera and M. Khan (2003)

9   G. Moher (2003)

10 Women on Farms (2003)

11 J.A. Flint (2003) 'Yum Brands Inc.', University of Oregon Investment Group, www.uoig.uoregon.edu/~uoig/reports/03Spring/YUM.pdf

12 P. Kaufman, C.R. Handy, E.W. Mclaughlin, K. Park, and G.M. Green (2000) 'Understanding the Dynamics of Produce Markets: Consumption and Consolidation Grow', USDA Economic Research Service, Agricultural Information Bulletin, No. 758

13 *The Grocer* (2003) 'Redrawing the grocery map of Britain', 11 January 2003

14 D. Weatherspoon and T. Reardon (2003) 'The rise of supermarkets in Africa: implications for agrifood systems and the rural poor', *Development Policy Review* 2003, May, 21 (3)

15 T. Reardon and J.A. Berdegué (2002) 'The rapid rise of supermarkets in Latin America: challenges and opportunities for development', *Development Policy Review* 2002, 20 (4): 371–88

16 M&M Planet Retail (2003) 'Top 30 grocery retailers worldwide 2002' www.planetretail.net

17 Cited in B. Vorley (2003) 'Food Inc. – Corporate Concentration from Farmer to Consumer', London: International Institute for Environment and Development

18 Women on Farms (2003)

19 Based on data for Granny Smith apples, at an exchange rate of rand 11 to £1

20 Oxfam interview October 2003

21 Oxfam interview October 2003

22 Women on Farms (2003)

23 B. Herrera et al. (2003)

24 Oxfam interview 23 October 2003

25 E. Díaz (2003)

26 C. Mather and S. Greenberg (2003)

27 Ibid.

28 Ibid.

29 Correspondence with South Africa Deciduous Fruit Producers Trust

30 P. Mattera and M. Khan (2003)

31 C. Mather and S. Greenberg (2003)

32 Competition Commission (2000) 'Supermarkets: a Report on the Supply of Groceries from Multiple Stores in the United Kingdom', Competition Commission Report 2000

33 Friends of the Earth Press Release: 'Supermarket Code Fails Farmers', 17 March 2003

34 EurepGap Protocol for Fresh Fruit and Vegetables 2001

35 D. Campbell (2003) 'Taco's tomato pickers on slave wages', *Guardian* 17 March 2003

36 B. Herrera et al. (2003)

37 C. Mather and S. Greenberg (2003)

38 S. Smith et al. (2003) op. cit.

39 Tesco (2003) Annual Report, www.tesco.com/r?from=HomepageCorp&url=/corporateinfo

40 Tesco Annual Reports 2002 and 2003. Data are: underlying diluted earnings per share, turnover excluding VAT, and underlying operating profit.

41 Tesco (2003) Annual Report

42 Tesco (2003) 'Every Little Helps: Corporate Social Responsibility Review', 2002–03

43 E-mail to Oxfam 2 December 2003

44 Ibid.

45 Interview with Oxfam 13 October 2003

46 Interview with Oxfam 25 September 2003

47 Interview with Oxfam 23 October 2003

48 Women on Farms (2003)

49 IGD (2003) Tesco Account Watch

50 Women on Farms (2003)

51 C. Mather, and S. Greenberg (2003)

52 Ibid.

53 Interview with Oxfam 23 October 2003

54 S. Kruger (2003) 'Interviews with seasonal women farm workers in South Africa'

55 C. Dolan and K. Sorby (2003) op. cit.

56 Ibid.

57 CEDEM (2003)

58 G. Moher (2003)

59 F. Brassel and C.E. Rangel (2001) op.cit.

60 B. Goldstein and J.B. Leonard (2003)

61 Ibid.

62 E. Díaz (2000) cited in CEDEM (2003)

63 CEDEM (2003)

64 A. du Toit and F. Ally (2001) cited in Women on Farms (2003)

65 C. Mather and S. Greenberg (2003)

66 A. du Toit (2003) cited in Women on Farms (2003)

67 Human Sciences Research Council (2002) cited in Women on Farms (2003)

68 UK House of Commons Environment Food and Rural Affairs Committee, 'Gangmasters', Fourteenth Report of Session, 2002–2003

69 S. Smith et al. (2003) op. cit

70 S. Barrientos and A. Barrientos (2002) 'Extending Social Protection to Informal Workers in the Horticulture Global Value Chain', Social Protection Discussion Paper Series, Washington D.C.: World Bank

71 CEDEM (2003)

72 B. Herrera et al. (2003)

73 Women on Farms (2003)

74 Coalition of Immokalee Workers, www.ciw-online.org

75 CEDEM (2003)

76 Ibid.

77 Ibid.

78 CACTUS (2001) cited in B. Herrera et al. (2003)

79 Interview by CACTUS 2001

80 Human Rights Watch (2000) 'Fingers to the Bone: United States Failure to Protect Child Farmworkers', www.hrw.org/reports/frmwrkr

81 US Department of Labor (2000) 'Findings of the National Agricultural Workers Survey (NAWS) 1997–98: A Demographic and Employment Profile of United States Farmworkers', Research Report No. 8, March, Washington, D.C.: US Department of Labor

82 B. Herrera et al. (2003)

83 S. Smith et al. (2003)

84 CEDEM (2003)

85 B. Herrera et al. (2003)

86 ICFTU (2003) op. cit

87 Women on Farms (2003)

88 CEDEM (2003)

Chapter 5

1 Oxfam interview 6 November 2003

2 ILO (2003) *Working Out of Poverty*, Geneva: ILO

3 Fair Wear Foundation (2002) 'Principles and Policies', Amsterdam: Fair Wear Foundation

4 Ethical Trading Initiative (2002) 'Principles of Implementation', www.eti.org.uk/pub/publications/purprinc/en/index.shtml

5 Oxfam interview 18 November 2003

6 Oxfam interview 20 November 2003

7 Oxfam interview 20 November 2003

8 Retailers Ethical Clothing Code of Practice, www.nosweatshoplabel.com

9 Social Investment Forum (2003) 'Report on Socially Responsible Investing Trends in the United States', wwwsocialinvest.org

10 Social Investment Organisation, www.socialinvestment.ca/AboutSIO.htm

11 EUROSIF (2003) 'Socially Responsible Investment Among European Investors', 2003 Report, www.eurosif.org

12 Social Investment Forum. op. cit.

13 www.fairtradefederation.com/ab_facts.html (May 2003)